DATE DUE

NO 3 0 '92	AP 23 '97		
JA 29 '93	MR 6 '98		
MR 1 9 '93	MY 26 '98		
MY 28 '93			
	FE 2 2 '99		
MR 1 8 '94	SE 3 0 '99		
	OC 2 0 '99		
JE 3 0 '94	NO 8 '99		
	FE 1 00		
OC 7 '94	MY 5 00		
FE 1 7 '95	DE 1 8 01		
NO 2 7 '95	MR 26 '02		
FE 2 3 '96	AP 1 7 04		
MR 2 2 '96	MY 9 05		
RENEW	OC 1 8 10		
SE 1 1 '96			
DE 1 0 '96			

DEMCO 38-296

Codependency

Kay Marie Porterfield

THE ROSEN PUBLISHING GROUP, INC./NEW YORK

Published in 1991 by The Rosen Publishing Group, Inc.
29 East 21st Street, New York, NY 10010

First Edition

Manufactured in the United States of America

Library of Congress Cataloging-in-Publication Data

Porterfield, Kay Marie.
    Coping with codependency / Kay Marie Porterfield.
        p.   cm.
    Includes bibliographical references and index.
    Summary: Discusses the meaning of codependency, in which
one individual depends upon another for emotional fulfillment,
and examines effective ways of dealing with this situation and
associated problems.
    ISBN 0-8239-1198-5
    1. Co-dependence (Psychology)—Juvenile literature.
[1. Co-dependence (Psychology)]   I. Title.
RC569.5.C63P67   1991
616.86—dc20
                                                    90-19879
                                                        CIP
                                                         AC

A B O U T   T H E   A U T H O R ◊

Kay Marie Porterfield has an MA degree in counseling and has been writing about addictions and relationships for thirteen years. Her articles have appeared in many national magazines. Her other books about dysfunctional families and addiction include *Keeping Promises: The Challenge of a Sober Parent*; *Violent Voices: Twelve Steps to Freedom from Emotional and Verbal Abuse*; and *Coping with an Alcoholic Parent*.

In addition to writing she has taught middle and high school English. Currently she teaches English and Journalism at Metropolitan State College in Denver, where she lives with her teenage son, Dylan, and her cat, Hobbit.

"I'm sure if I had known about the concept of codependency during my teenage years, my own growing pains wouldn't have hurt quite so much," she says. "Too often parents, teachers, and teenagers themselves believe that adolescence and suffering are one and the same. They don't have to be if we learn to accept and respect ourselves. Once we begin to listen to and heed the messages from our own heart, we stop depending on others to make us feel good about ourselves. We can move beyond merely surviving adolescence and start thriving."

For
my students past
and
present

Contents

Introduction: Codependent? Who, Me?

Codependency is a hot topic these days. It's discussed on TV talk shows and written about in many magazines. You may already know a little about the subject, but you still may be wondering if you *are* a codependent. The following checklist can help you decide. As you read the statements, see how many you agree with.

- Usually I have to work hard to earn the love and approval of people around me.
- Often I feel I'm not as good as others.
- When things go wrong it 's usually my fault.
- I'm afraid that if I make mistakes people won't like me.
- It seems as if I can't do anything right.
- I can figure out what other people need to be happy, but I don't know what I need.
- My friends and family often guess how I feel before I know.
- Most of the time it's dangerous to express one's true feelings.
- Other people won't like me if I disagree with them.
- I try not to cause trouble by saying what I really think.

- The best way to get through life is to keep a smile on your face no matter what.
- Anger and arguments make me very uncomfortable.
- When people do me favors, I think they want something.
- It's always better to be a giver than a taker.
- When people compliment me, I rarely believe them.
- I don't need anything from anybody.
- Most of the time I have a hard time getting close to people.
- When I'm dating or with my friends, I feel trapped.
- Often I find myself doing things I don't want to do to make other people happy.
- I stay in dating relationships and friendships even though I no longer like the people I'm involved with.
- Many of my relationships have ended in pain.
- I feel responsible for solving other people's problems.
- My friends and family rely on me for advice.
- Often I "catch" moods from those around me the way some people catch colds.
- One of the things I fear most is rejection.
- Most of my friends need me for the help I give them.
- I hate being alone.
- It seems to me that my life is controlled by other people's feelings, wishes, and needs.
- The best way to get people to do what you want is to manipulate or bribe them.
- The only way my life is going to improve is when my friends and family members change.
- I have difficulty having fun.
- It's hard for me to relax.

√ • There isn't enough time in a day to do all the things I need to do.

√ • I worry more than most people.

Although there is no magical score that qualifies you as a codependent, your responses to this checklist can give you some clues.

If you agreed with several of the statements, that's a hint that you are more than a little unhappy with yourself and the direction your life is taking. Maybe you have become a doormat that people walk all over. Perhaps you have become a martyr, offering to sacrifice your own needs for other people. You may have a hard time with relationships, either smothering people or pushing them away. Or maybe you never know what you feel and you rely on other people to give you hints.

All teenagers have bouts of self-doubt and occasionally live their lives based on what others think of them. Codependent teenagers, on the other hand, suffer from intense feelings of insecurity and spend most of their time and energy seeking approval from others. They do that because they don't know how else to cope with life. Even though those of us who are codependent may seem to be doing fine on the outside, our self-doubts are so many and so huge that we feel miserable and resentful most of the time.

If you have experienced any of the codependency symptoms on the list, you know they're worse than no fun—they're painful! Whether your codependency is mild or severe, you would probably like to change how you feel by taking charge of your life, if only you knew how. That is what this book is all about—changing yourself and the way you interact with people around you. It is about finding out who you are and finding the freedom to be yourself. By reading the chapters that follow and doing the suggested exercises, you can gain a set of tools for becoming your own person.

Who needs the misery of codependency? Certainly not you!

CHAPTER 1

Will the Real Codependent Please Stand Up?

Marti has been dating Fred for a whole year even though he never makes plans in advance and sometimes drinks so much that she has to get friends to drive her home from parties. He is failing his junior year and has lost his after-school job. Lately Marti has been doing his homework and paying for their dates. She suspects that he's seeing other girls while she does his algebra and writes his essays. That bothers her, but still she sticks with him. "He needs me," she says. "I know I can help him get his act together. When he does, everything will be fine. Besides, I don't know if I could get another boyfriend. Maybe no other boy will ever be interested in me."

Since Guy's parents were divorced three years ago, his mother has been depressed. As her only child, he feels responsible for cheering her up. She relies on him to do the grocery shopping, the houscleaning, and the car repairs. Although she has a job, she has no friends. He resents her expectation that he'll spend all his free time with her, and he hates it when she says mean things about his father. But he keeps his feelings to himself. After all, now he's the man of the house, and he believes that his mother couldn't survive without him. Lately, though, no matter how hard he tries, he always seems to mess up. In the space of two months, he has been late for school six mornings and misplaced his homework twice. To make matters worse, he forgot to check the oil in the car, which caused extensive engine damage.

When Bev's classmates see her walking down the hall, they snicker and turn away. At first it hurt because she wanted more than anything to be popular. Now she has adjusted. If she has no friends, that's fine with her. "Who needs them?" she says bitterly. "People just get close to you to find out ways to hurt you." To protect herself, Bev dresses unattractively and reads con-stantly, rarely looking up from her book. Next to her science fiction novels, eating is her only pleasure. Over the past two years she has gained fifty pounds. When her gym teacher suggested that she go on a diet, Bev flew into a rage. At home, though, she cried for hours and even thought about suicide—until her mother cheered her up with a cheesecake and a pan of brownies.

Not so long ago teenagers like Marti, Guy, and Bev would have been told that their misery was a normal part of adolescence, something they would outgrow. At worst, they were going through an awkward stage. When they became adults they would look back and laugh at the troubles they had in high school. Today we know better. The problems and negative feelings these teenagers are experiencing are more than just growing pains; they are part of an emotional disorder that counselors call codependency. And codependency is no laughing matter.

Even though people have denied their feelings and compulsively taken care of others since the beginning of recorded history, the term *codependency* is fairly recent. In fact, it was only a few years ago that addiction counselors began noticing something very interesting as they worked with alcoholics and their families. They discovered that people who live with chemically dependent relatives share many of the same ways of relating to the world even though they come from very different families.

After years of adjusting to life with a family member who is an alcoholic or a drug addict, people go through a number of changes to survive in one piece. Often they:

- Keep the family problem a secret from the outside world;
- Take care of the troubled person;
- Learn to pretend that everything is fine no matter what is going on;
- Blame themselves for their relative's problem;
- Believe that all their problems would be solved if only their loved one would get better;
- Rigidly relate to other people the way they relate to the problem person in their family.

Even though these coping styles work within their families, the people who use them feel ashamed, angry, and sad. In the outside world those same attitudes and tactics, which the counselors named codependency, often fail completely. It is not only the substance abuser who needs help; his or her whole family does.

As time went by and therapists compared notes, they discovered that many people who did not come from substance-abusing families acted just like those who did. If you were raised in a family where someone had an eating disorder such as bulimia or anorexia, if one of your parents was depressed or angry much of the time, you had a major chance of growing up to be a codependent.

Soon professionals began using the term *dysfunctional family* to talk about alcohol- or drug-abusing families or any family that does not meet the needs of its members. These are families that do not support each member's sense of well-being and do not allow emotional growth. They do not function as healthy families.

Some dysfunctional families have major problems such as incest or battering. Others struggle with less obvious troubles such as shame over having a gay relative or the pain and anger of divorce. Today it is generally accepted that your family need not have severe problems for you to become codependent; your family's stress can be hidden. Having a parent who is a workaholic and who ignores you can set you up for codependency. So can having parents who often yell at you although they may never slap or hit you. Perhaps your parents usually give you love and attention, but a death in the family, a long-term illness, or money troubles have triggered stressful conditions that create codependency.

You are at high risk for becoming a codependent if you:

- were sexually abused;
- were battered;

- were neglected;
- were emotionally or verbally abused;
- live with an alcohol or drug abuser;
- are an alcohol or drug abuser;
- live in a family that has experienced a great deal of stress;
- live in a family with a secret.

CODEPENDENCY TRAITS

People who grow up in troubled and stressful families do not all react to their upbringing in the same way. If you asked your brother or sister to answer the codependency checklist, chances are their answers would differ from yours. Despite their differences, however, codependents do share many common behaviors and beliefs.

Low Self-esteem: "I'm Not Good Enough."

Brian is a handsome fifteen-year-old. He gets Bs and Cs in his classes, is on the track team, and holds a part-time job bussing tables in a Mexican restaurant. Even though he has plenty of friends and is well liked by his teachers, he feels rotten about himself. He thinks that if he could get better grades, work longer hours, and have more friends, he would be a success as a teenager.

No matter how many awards we win or compliments we receive, we codependents tend to put ourselves down constantly. No matter how hard we try, we never feel that we're good enough, smart enough, or good-looking enough. Often our low self-esteem turns into shame. Like Brian, we are convinced that our actions do not measure up, and we're sure *we* don't measure up as human beings. Since we believe we are so messed up and we feel helpless to change, we try to hide the secret of who we really are from our friends, our family, and even from ourselves.

Denial of Emotions: "I Don't Feel a Thing."

Ever since Karen can remember, her father has carried on affairs. When she was little she couldn't figure out why her parents rarely spoke to each other. Now that she is older she knows the cause of all the silence and bitterness in her house. She can't recall a time when her parents got along. She wishes they would get a divorce, but they claim they're staying together for her sake. Because she is helpless to change how they feel about each other, she goes through life pretending that her family is no different from anyone else's. "It doesn't matter to me that they don't love each other," she tells herself. "Their problems don't affect me a bit." But she has stomachaches and tension headaches almost every day.

When we are codependent, we're so busy trying to escape from our anger, shame, and pain that we have trouble knowing what we feel. On the surface we're numb, but deeper inside our feelings eat away at us. Whether a codependent feels frightened or sad or enraged, he or she will smile, even though it is phony. Ask a codependent what is wrong and you'll probably get a shrug and be told, "Oh, nothing. Everything's fine." And that is what a codependent believes, although it is not true. As codependents we are so out of touch with our feelings and so used to denying our own needs that we may even forget the meaning behind the names for emotions. Just having convinced ourselves that we're feeling no pain doesn't mean that we don't have pain locked away inside.

Communication Problems: "I Don't Want to Talk about It."

Robin was upset when her history teacher made a mistake averaging her midsemester grades and gave her a D rather than the C she had earned. She thought about telling him before he turned in the grades to the office and they went on the report cards, but she was afraid. Sure, Mr. Roth had always been nice to her, but she didn't want to put him to any trouble. Besides, he might think she was a complainer. So she kept quiet, but she decided he had done it purposely because he hated her and thought she was stupid. She had such trouble paying attention the rest of the semester that she wound up failing his class.

Since codependents often are not aware of what we're feeling or even what we want or need, we have a tough time expressing those feelings and needs. Even when we do figure out what is wrong and try to talk about it, we often can't find the right words. When we do find words, they may come out in a confusing jumble. Sometimes we even say the opposite of what we mean, afraid that if our friends or family knew our true feelings, they wouldn't like us. Most of the time we keep our thoughts and feelings to ourselves and expect other people to read our minds. When they don't, we simmer with resentment. This lack of communication not only keeps us from getting what we want but also makes relationships with others very difficult.

Emotional Intimacy Problems: "Go Away Closer!"

Steve is a regular comedian in his classes. When he tells jokes, he gets a big laugh. He uses his sense of humor to charm girls and has no trouble getting dates. But asking a girl out a third or fourth time scares him half to death. He would like to have a steady girlfriend, but he's certain that once a girl figured out that his stand-up comic role is just an act, that he's really shy, she would dump him. So he turns sarcastic and dumps her first—before she has a chance to hurt him.

Because codependents are afraid of being hurt, it's almost impossible for us to maintain healthy long-term friendships or to feel emotionally close to people. Like Steve, we're terrified that they might see behind our "Everything's okay" mask and learn our secret feelings. Then they might reject us. As little kids, most codependents learned not to trust others, because too often trusting meant getting hurt. Since our self-esteem is shaky to begin with, we do not want to risk loving and losing. If our family or friends got angry with us, how would we survive? Even though we may desperately want relationships, we often put up a wall to keep others away at the very time we're begging them be our friends.

Living Though Others: "I'm Nobody until Somebody Loves Me."

Terry's best friend, Beth, takes advantage of her every chance she gets. When Terry lends Beth money, she isn't paid back. Beth borrows her sweaters and returns them stained. She steals things and expects Terry to lie for her. Lately Beth has been experimenting with drugs and urging Terry to smoke joints in the bathroom at school. Why does Terry put up with the trouble her best friend brings into her life? She is convinced that Beth, whose mother is an alcoholic, needs her support. "I couldn't abandon her," she says. "I'm the only thing keeping her out of trouble." In truth, Terry is afraid that without Beth she would be friendless.

Despite our walls, codependents are people who need people. To make sure that others like us, we become people pleasers. We would rather be the givers than the takers, whether of compliments, offers of help, or presents. We measure our worth by the people around us: If they approve of us, we must be okay; if not, something is wrong with us. When Beth is angry, Terry thinks it must be her fault; something she has said or done has upset her friend. Since what other people want is more important to us than our own needs, we'll do anything to manipulate their feelings—even things that are against our own values such as using drugs. As Terry did, we fall into the trap of thinking we can fix other people. We pick up the pieces for them while our own lives are falling apart.

Powerlessness: "What's the Use of Trying?"

Joe is in a slump. He has been in one since sixth grade. That's when his father and his uncles started putting pressure on him to play basketball. They had all played in high school and even in college. Joe is tall enough and fairly coordinated. The only problem is that he *hates* the sport; he'd rather swim. Over the years he and his father have waged one battle after another over Joe's refusal to try out for the team. When it seemed that his father wouldn't love him if he didn't follow in his fooststeps, Joe went on strike. Now he's a couch potato. If nothing he does makes Dad happy with him, why do anything except change channels?

When we live through other people and look for approval from them, we're bound to feel powerless. In effect, we give away our power to other people, so that we go through life feeling like victims. Sometimes we let our powerlessness paralyze us. At other times we may be so confused about what we want to do that we have a terrible time making decisions. It's easier to stop trying, to ask others to tell us what to do, or to convince ourselves that they're forcing us do things against our wills and ruining our lives. In many situations we react to pressures out-side ourselves rather than acting on our own needs and wishes. Like puppets, we let our family and friends pull our strings.

Addictions and Compulsions: "I'm Looking for Love in All the Wrong Places."

For as long as she can remember, Jennifer has been tormented by an empty ache inside. It seems to her that her parents have always paid more attention to her brother and her sister. Her mother even told her that she was a mistake, that there were already enough kids in the family when Jennifer was born. Although her mother spends little time with her daughter, she tries to make up for it by giving Jennifer money. Several years ago Jennifer found out that shopping made her feel better, at least for a while.

The thrill of finding the perfect blouse or a great new cosmetic gave her a high. Now she spends all her free time at the mall, and her closet is full of clothing she will never wear.

Many codependent teenagers look for temporary ways to boost their self-esteem, dull their painful feelings, and fill their emptiness. They turn to activities, to people, or even to drugs and alcohol to try to make up for the love they didn't get when they were younger or may not be getting today. Although things outside of us can make us feel better for a while, their effect soon wears off and we need more. We get so hooked on shopping or bowling or studying that those things rule our lives. Sometimes we get stuck in destructive and addictive friendships or love relationships, unable to let go and to grow, or we may get tangled up with drugs and alcohol. Because codependents get so caught up in running away from themselves, we don't find the permanent solutions to our emptiness that lie inside of us.

Going to Extremes: "When I'm Good, I'm Very, Very Good—When I'm Bad I'm Horrid."

Barry's teachers say he drives them crazy. For weeks at a time he does all his homework and stays up all night to check it over. Then he gets fed up with trying to be the perfect student and doesn't do any assignments for a while. Sometimes he admires his teachers and is super-friendly to them. At other times he hates them, sitting through classes glaring at them and giving sullen responses to questions. He is never in the middle, and nobody can figure out what he'll do next—least of all Barry!

Codependents go from one extreme to the other. We try so hard to win approval that we burn out and then don't try at all. Since we hold our negative feelings inside while we keep a smile on our faces for the world, we often blow up over little things. We go for weeks doing what we think we should, and then we do everything we know we shouldn't. First we cling to people because we want to be close, then without warning we push away, afraid of being hurt. Our sudden switches in mood, behavior, and beliefs are as confusing to us as they are to others. Because we live on the outside, we don't know ourselves.

In the final analysis, codependency is a problem of relationships—relationship to ourselves, to other people, and to the things outside of us that we compulsively try to substitute for self-love. Instead of acting from the authentic core of who we are. we live our lives based on what other people think about us. Instead of meeting our own needs, we always try to meet the needs of others. Instead of learning to love ourselves, we demand love from others. Because we feel so powerless, we manipulate and try to control their lives instead of gaining control of our own.

To cure our codependency, we need to turn our focus on ourselves and find out who we are. We need to learn to love ourselves and to live from the inside out, meeting our own needs and taking charge of what happens in our lives.

CHAPTER 2

Codependency: What It Is and Isn't

L iving for ourselves *sounds* simple enough. After all, how tough can it to be take an honest look at our attitudes and behavior? Or to learn about new and healthy ways of coping and finally to practice them? It can be *very* tough if you're a codependent!

Change is overwhelming for anyone. It is especially difficult for codependents because we become very worried if life isn't orderly and predictable. The whole point of our codependent behavior is to survive the stress and chaos in our families when we are growing up. Even though today our codependency makes us miserable, we know what to expect—the worst. We may shudder at the thought of changing and facing the unknown, even though we're fairly sure life could be better if we took that risk.

To change from being codependents into fully functioning humans means to accept ourselves, to feel, to trust, to talk, to grow—exactly the things we were taught *not* to do when we were kids. Not surprisingly, codependents can come up with dozens of ways to talk themselves out of breaking free from their codependency. Here are just a few common excuses.

TEN MYTHS OF CODEPENDENCY

Myth One: "I must have been born this way"

Codependents are made, not born! Hiding from ourselves and depending on things outside for our self-esteem were lessons taught in childhood. Because our codependency is something we learned one lesson at a time, we can unlearn it one lesson at a time.

Myth Two: "Give me time, I'll outgrow it"

As we said before, all teenagers experience some of the symptoms of codependency some of the time. Rather than moving through the sometimes hard lessons of the teen years, codependents stay stuck. We may get hooked on one obessive relationship after another, sacrificing our own happiness to gain approval, or build a wall to keep everyone away. If your adolescence seems far more painful than that of teenagers you know, if you feel unhappy with yourself most of the time, you can take a chance on letting your codependency cure itself, or you can take charge and do something about it now. Codependency is not just another growing pain, and it does not miraculously disappear the day you turn twenty-one.

Myth Three: "Codependency is a disease with no cure"

The word codependency sounds pretty serious—as though it were a fatal curse or an incurable disease. It is not. Because codependency is a survival skill, a set of relationship patterns and attitudes that you learned, you can unlearn them. Codependency is a set of coping habits that no longer work for you. Breaking bad habits takes effort, but it can be done.

Myth Four: "Why does everybody pick on me?"

Since codependents blame themselves for everything that goes wrong in the world, you may feel that being labeled a codependent is just another way of fingerpointing. It isn't. You didn't ask to be raised in a family that taught you to be codependent, so becoming a codependent *was not* your fault. Choosing to remain stuck in codependency *is* a conscious choice for which you are responsible.

Myth Five: "I must be crazy"

Absolutely not! As a codependent you may do things that make no sense to people outside of your dysfunctional family but make perfect sense to its members. As you move toward independence and leaving home, as you form relationships with friends, classmates, teachers, bosses, coworkers, and boyfriends and girlfriends, it becomes painfully obvious that codependency is not working. It no longer meets your needs, and it is making you miserable. Feeling bad isn't the same as being crazy. Calling codependency craziness is a way of giving in to it and getting out of doing anything about it.

Myth Six: "Since my family did this to me, they're responsible for fixing me"

Although it is true that you were not born codependent and did not volunteer for the title, expecting your parents to solve your codependency problems for you is a good example of codependent thinking. In the first place, the people you live with are probably doing the best they can. They may lack the emotional resources or the background to give you the help you need to break the codependency cycle. In the second place, you can't make others change against their will. The cure for codependency comes from inside. No matter how the problem started, *you* are the only one who can learn to feel your own feelings and to express them. You are the only one who can teach yourself to live from the inside out.

Myth Seven: "There's nothing wrong with me a new boyfriend or girlfriend won't cure"

As codependents, we like to look outside of ourselves for solutions. If our family can't do it, we tell ourselves, there must be somebody who can make our codependency go away. So we often search for a romantic partner and believe that he or she can give us all the love our family couldn't. If the girlfriend or boyfriend we choose is not a codependent, the relationship may work for a time, but soon our old codependency, patterns reassert themselves. There is no way that other people, no matter how much they love us, can make up to us for an unhappy childhood. Before we can love others, really love them, we need to learn to love ourselves.

Myth Eight: "I'll have to give up being in love"

If by love you mean clinging and whining and demanding that other people make you feel better about yourself, then, yes, you'll need to give it up along with your codependency. Once you have discarded those outdated ideas about love, you'll discover new ones such as caring based on mutual trust and emotional intimacy. You'll find out that people love you for yourself rather than the act you put on. And next time somebody gives you a present, you can enjoy it without feeling so guilty that you rush out to buy him or her a bigger one.

Myth Nine: "When I get rid of codependency, I'll be a mean and selfish person"

No way! You'll be a whole person instead of a person with a big empty hole inside, and you'll have a lot more to give to other people than you do now. Codependents may seem to be generous, but most of the time we do not give freely of ourselves. Instead, we try to trade our time and affection for positive self-esteem to fill that empty space inside of us.

Myth Ten: "I can't help myself"

Of course you can't—not when you're too busy helping everybody else in your life. Counselors call our "Why try?" attitude *learned helpness*. After spending time in a dysfunctional family, we learn that trying to change things is useless. Chances are, however, that when we learned to give up and give in we were focusing on changing other people rather than ourselves. We are the only people we can change. Once we learn to focus on ourselves, we can fix ourselves.

If you have fallen into the trap of believing these myths, chances are that on some level your codependency is working for you rather than against you. Maybe you enjoy the attention you receive when you feel and act helpless and hopeless. When Marsha's boss criticizes her for not doing her job right at the shoestore where she works on weekends, she bursts into tears. She is trying as hard as she can, she tells him; it's just that her mother is having surgery and her brother is in trouble with the law and her father has a drinking problem. The manager always apologizes and offers to buy her a soda. Because Marsha has his pity, she's fairly certain she won't be fired. On the other hand, she does not have his respect and will probably never be promoted.

Perhaps when you give up your own needs to make other people happy or to fix them up, you feel superior to them. Ben has run a three-year campaign to reform his older sister, who became pregnant when she was in high school and then married and divorced—all before she was eighteen. He tells her how to raise her young son, criticizes the way she spends her money, and leaves religious tracts at her apartment when he baby-sits for her. Sure, he resents the insults she gives him for his efforts, but he also gets an ego boost from his actions. After all, he's the good kid in the family, and she's the bad one. At home, remembering that fact helps him through the times when his father curses at him and calls him stupid.

Maybe codependency gives you an excuse to blame other people for everything that's wrong with your life. LaDonna *would* go to art school when she gets out of high school if her father could hold down a steady job. If he was bringing home more money for diet food, maybe she could lose some weight. Probably her grades would be better, too, if she had brand-new textbooks rather than used ones. She knows that boys would ask her out if she had a whole new wardrobe and could change her hairdo. It just isn't fair, she grumbles. If only he'd get a decent job, everything would change...everything. Feeling sorry for ourselves and grumbling, without ever doing anything about our problems, is sometimes easier than taking responsibility for changing what we can.

Before you get ready to give up your old way of relating to yourself and to the world, it's important to understand just what you are getting yourself into. Or to put it another way:

CODEPENDENCY

IS	and	ISN'T
Staying stuck		Growing
Taking care of		Caring about
Needing people		Choosing to be with people
Self-hatred		Self-love
Dependence		Independence
Confusion		Knowing what you feel
Stuffing feelings		Saying how you feel
Mind reading		Asking and listening
Manipulating		Expressing wants and needs
Resenting		Saying no
Being passive		Being active
Giving up power		Self-empowerment
Hiding the real you		Sharing the real you
Being a doormat		Setting boundaries
Denial and dishonesty		Facing facts
Bossing and controlling		Tolerance
Keeping grudges		Forgiving
Being rigid		Staying flexible
Feeling shame		Feeling self-confidence
Worrying		Making decisions
Blaming		Being responsible
Waiting to be rescued		Taking charge of your future

Will you remain codependent, or will you change? The choice is entirely up to you. Just as it is impossible for you to wave a magic wand and transform other people into what you want them to be, it is also impossible for another person—or a book—to wave a magic wand over you and create lasting change. Books and people help, but you are the one with the magic wand. It's your heartfelt desire to change the way you think about yourself and how you interact with others that works the magic.

Of course, you *could* decide that you really like being a codependent. Maybe you don't want to change. That's okay, too. You'll stop being codependent when *you* are good and ready, which is a good thing. Deciding to change your life because a book tells you to, even though you don't feel the need to change, is (you guessed it!) codependency.

CHAPTER ◇ 3

Why Codependency Happens

Before we can move ahead to healing our codependency, we need to look back to find out where it came from. You already know that codependency is a *learned* pattern of feeling and behaving, and that you weren't born that way. Even through we were taught by our experiences to live outside ourselves very early in life, we didn't choose it as we would choose to sign up for a course in algebra or French. Instead we simply happened to be born into families where codependency was already a way of life. As we grew up, codependency was the main coping skill we saw others use, and we were encouraged to use it ourselves. If we had not become codependent, we would not have fit into our families. Being part of a family is critical to your day-to-day survival, especially when you're a little kid.

Nobody's family is perfect. Some families, though, are better for children's emotional health than others. As we said earlier, the big problem with dysfunctional families is that they don't meet the needs of their members. To grow emotionally, children require many things. To become well-adjusted adults, kids need:

- Food, clothing, shelter, and medical care.
  (All your physical needs are met.)
- Acceptance, belonging, love, friendship.
  (Your parents love you for who you are, spend time with you, and encourage you to have friends.)
- Safety, security, order, protection.
  (Life at home runs fairly smoothly and peacefully.)
- Acknowledgment.
  (Your opinions count at home, and you receive compliments.)
- Discipline and guidance.
  (Your parents set consistent and fair limits on your behavior.)
- Independence, privacy, personal fulfillment, and growth.
  (Within reasonable limits, you're encouraged to be yourself and to think and act for yourself.)

Some parents do not or cannot provide their children with enough to eat, decent clothing, and a place to live. Others never really wanted children, are not happy with the kids they have, or are just too busy to be parents. Parents whose own lives are turned upside down by addictions or emotional problems cannot provide a peaceful, safe, and predictable home for their children. Many of our parents were not raised very well themselves and so do not know how to help their children feel important. There are parents who don't know how to set rules for their children and parents who make so many rules that their kids feel like prisoners.

When we belong to families like these, we tend to get emotionally stuck at the age and stage of development at which our needs were not being met. Although we grow up on the outside, inside it's a different story—we're still needy. Since our parents did not meet our needs, we turn other people into substitute parents whom we try to manipulate into filling those unmet needs. Many of us have no idea what security, self-confidence, or self-love feel like because we have never experienced them before. We are completely convinced that the only way we can feel those good emotions is for a friend or a date or even a teacher to give them to us desperately believing that we need others to make us happy.

In fact, we are so desperate that we cling, demand, and try to coax people to make us feel good about ourselves. We may persuade them to try to fill our empty space, but they never can, for long. We end up feeling angry and more unloved than ever. That is when many codependents turn to drugs, alcohol, and other addictions. Something has to make us feel better, we tell ourselves. We may suspect that *we* can, but even so we don't know how.

Often we go about living a lot like two-year-olds struggling to be independent. We hang on to other people, then blow up and push them away, only to come back and hang on even more tightly. We are good little boys and girls for a while; then we throw tantrums. No wonder that toddler time of life is called the Terrible Twos. Because we were never allowed to complete that stage of emotional growth, we may be two years old inside.

In fact, some psychologists talk about the codependent's inner child, the emotional part of us that got frozen in time because we were not given the tools we needed to grow up. Even though many of us codependents appear and act older and more mature than our real age, on the inside that little kid is still crying, pleading, and throwing temper tantrums to get its needs met.

WHY SOME PARENTS DON'T MEET THEIR KIDS' NEEDS

Dysfunctional families are not all alike because the people who make them up are not alike. Families that don't meet kids' needs come in all shapes, sizes, and colors. They're found at all social and economic levels, too. Many dysfunctional families look very good from the outside: The parents have super jobs, and the kids have great clothes and belong to all the right clubs. Outsiders do not understand the emotional pain and loneliness that can go on behind closed doors. Just because a family looks healthy doesn't mean that its members have no problems; they may just be good at hiding them.

Some parents in dysfunctional families are able to meet some of their children's needs. They may not be able to provide much security, but they can and do give attention. Or they allow their kids little independence, but they do provide discipline. Even when parents can meet very few of their children's needs, grandparents, aunts, uncles, neighbors, and older siblings may be able to give us some of the necessary love and attention. As a general rule, the more your emotional needs were met when you were little, the milder your codependence will be today.

Few parents deprive their kids on purpose. The families that foster codependence are not *bad* families in the sense that parents planned to have children and decided at the same time not to meet their needs. Often parents love their children deeply and do the best they can for them, but some of these parents do not know how to provide for their children emotionally because their own needs were not met when they were growing up. Other parents have such problem-filled lives that they lack the emotional strength or energy to cope fully with the responsibilities of raising kids. Following are the most common reasons for parents' failure to meet their children's needs.

Their Parents Were Codependent

Maybe your grandparents were codependent and passed it on to their children, your parents. Codependency problems tend to run in families for generation after generation. Even though your mother and father may be free of addiction and free of major stresses, they may not be free of codependency. Parents cannot teach their kids to cope with life in healthy ways if they do not know how to do it themselves. Neither can they show us how to have self-esteem or how to get along with others if they were never taught or learned them on their own.

Jeannie's mother is always fishing for compliments. If her daughter doesn't constantly notice and praise her, she gets upset, says Jeannie doesn't love her, and cries. In a lot of ways Jeannie has to be her mother's parent, giving her the reassurance she never got as a child. In fact, Jeannie's grandma is still overcritical to the point of being nasty, not only to her daughter but to Jeannie as well. It is not unusual for her to call up and complain about something said or done years ago.

Even though Jeannie knows her grandma was abandoned as a child and had to live with a relative who molested her, that does not help Jeannie much. She feels sorry for her grandma and wants to make her mother feel okay about herself because she loves her. But sometimes she wonders if anyone will ever pay attention to her or reassure her about herself. She feels the emotional weight of her family on her shoulders and longs for the day she'll find a boyfriend who can make *her* feel cared for.

A Family Member Is Addicted

Children's needs are usually a low priority when a family member suffers from an addiction. Even if your parents are fine, a brother's or sister's addiction will affect your family in a negative way. Some people are addicted to alcohol or drugs, but others can be addicted to activities.

Chuck's older brother has always loved to gamble. Often he spends his whole paycheck placing bets that never pay off. Instead of buying Chuck a real present for his birthday, his brother bought him fifty lottery tickets and then insisted on buying more tickets with the twenty-dollar winnings. Even though he says he can quit gambling any time, he is addicted to it, and his whole family is so hurt by it that they can think of little else. Their lives are filled with working and saving money to pay off his debts as well as hiding their problem from relatives and neighbors.

In addition to gambling, people can be hooked on such activities as shopping, eating, having love affairs, working — or even sewing, going to church, or collecting cars. No matter what their addiction, they're happy only when they're doing that activity. As their obsession gets bigger and bigger, other parts of their life shrink smaller and smaller in importance to them. The addicted person finally becomes so caught up with the substance or activity that his or her whole life revolves around it.

A Family Member Is Being Sexually Abused

Usually we assume that sexual abuse means unwanted physical contact with a family member. Kids who are forced into sexual relationships and become victims of incest are betrayed by the very people they love and trust the most. When a parent or another family member is abusing you sexually, there is no way your need for security or safety can be met. Neither can you meet your need for privacy — not when your very body is violated and you have no control over what is happening to you. The shame of being invaded by sexual abuse is so powerful that it can be emotionally crippling.

Incest need not involve touching. Sexual abuse can be psychological and have as many negative effects as physical molestation. When a parent makes fun of your developing body or won't give you privacy in the bathroom, that is an invasion of your sexual boundaries. So is being turned into a substitute husband or wife for your parent, because it places you in a role that is not healthy for you to play.

Monica's mother has been ill with muscular dystrophy for a long time. For the last two years she has been confined to a wheelchair, so Monica has taken over most of the household duties: cooking, cleaning, shopping, and caring for her younger sister and brother. As the mother's health continues to worsen, fourteen-year-old Monica has become her father's best friend. He confides all his worries to her, and sometimes the two of them stay up so late talking that Monica can't do her schoolwork. She gives him back-rubs, cooks his favorite meals, and tries to tell him jokes. He calls her his little wife and the woman of the house. All of Monica's friends are starting to be interested in boys, but her father is so jealous of her time and attention that he won't even let her talk to boys on the phone. Even though he has never touched her sexually or even hinted at it, the way he relates to her is keeping her from learning to develop healthy love relationships with the opposite sex.

Physical Abuse Is Taking Place

Families that batter are dysfunctional, too. When Roger's father gets angry, he takes off his belt and beats his wife. He used to beat Roger until the teenager threatened to hit him back. Now Roger's stomach is in knots most of the time because he feels he should protect his mother but is afraid to. She stays in the marriage because she's afraid to leave and is not sure she could support herself and her son. "I'll divorce him when you leave home," she tells Roger. That makes him feel guilty beyond words. Both mother and son live in terror of the father's uncontrollable rages, and they try to be invisible when he's home. Nobody outside the family suspects the fear and anger Roger and his mother feel because the father is well respected in the community; in fact, he's a Sunday School teacher.

Punching, kicking, slapping, shoving, beating, stabbing, and shooting are all forms of physical abuse whether they come from a parent or any other relative—including brothers and sisters. So are unnecessarily forceful spankings. Unfortunately, many parents today do batter their children or each other. According to recent estimates, battering occurs in one out of five families. Even if you escape being the target of a family member's rage, witnessing the beating of a relative can have a negative effect on you, as it does for Roger. You may come to believe that the violence is your fault, or you may learn to be terrified of anger.

The Family Is Emotionally Abusive

Emotional abuse is even more widespread than battering. All of us lose our temper once in a while, saying and doing things we wish we hadn't, but emotional abusers make a habit of it. They rage and storm over even the smallest irritations, and it is impossible to predict when they will lose their temper. The scars left by this verbal violence are invisible, but they hurt deeply just the same.

> When Tina's mother is angry at her daughter for coming home even ten minutes late, she calls her a slut and a whore in a voice loud enough for all the neighbors to hear. Several times she has told Tina that she was a big mistake and should never have been born. Once she even tore up Tina's best clothes, the ones she wore for special occasions. After these big outbursts, however, she is extra nice, giving her daughter money and taking her places. Although her mother has never hit her, Tina feels confused, unloved, and ashamed. No matter how hard she tries to please, nothing works. More and more often Tina believes that maybe she *is* just a mistake.

Name-calling, threats of physical abuse, put-downs, and temper tantrums are all forms of verbal abuse. So is sarcasm; you don't need to be yelled at to be completely humiliated. Some emotional abusers operate by being controlling. They may ground their children for months at a time or arrange friendships for them. Other emotional abusers throw tantrums when their kids make friends outside the family. Anything that threatens their total control may trigger an emotional attack.

The Family Has a Secret

Families usually try to hide addictions and physical, sexual, and verbal abuse from outsiders. They are ashamed of their problem, often too ashamed even to seek help.

Other secrets that families keep are just as damaging even though not as "big" as addiction or abuse. Often these deep, dark mysteries are kept from people *inside* the family out of an overwhelming sense of shame. Even though the family secrets are never spoken aloud, they grow more and more powerful. The secret could be that a relative several generations back committed suicide, or someone in the family was born before the parents were married. Often, however, the secrets are not nearly so spectacular. Maybe a parent was previously married, or a child has been adopted. The damaging thing about secrets often is not the secret itself but how the family feels about it.

Some parents keep secrets from their kids because they believe it is for the children's good. Jason's father lost his executive position when his company was sold. Even though his bad luck had nothing to do with the quality of his work, he felt that he was a failure and kept his firing from his kids. Every morning he left the house at the usual time and returned at dinnertime.

Jason knew something was wrong because his father was so nervous and irritable, but no one would talk about it. He watched as his mother started taking tranquilizers and drinking. All of a sudden his parents, who had always been generous, cut off his allowance and refused to discuss his college plans. Jason blamed himself for their change in attitude and for the tension in the house. He felt that he had to walk on eggshells. Not knowing the truth was hurting him more than having to face unpleasant facts and cope with them. At least then he wouldn't feel responsible for his family situation.

The Family Is Undergoing Major Stress

Finally, stress, even when it's out in the open, can make an ordinarily healthy family start to fall apart at the seams. Often the tension is nobody's fault; it just happens. A relative dies. The family moves to another state. Parents divorce and then remarry. A child is born with a birth defect and requires constant care. Each of these events can unbalance a family. In fact, any major change, good or bad, will cause emotional strain on family members. The more changes a family confronts and the bigger those changes are, the higher the stress level.

Ask Becky, whose mother inherited a bundle of money when her aunt died. Almost overnight the single mother and her daughter moved from a cramped apartment to a big house in a rich neighborhood. Becky transferred to a private school and traded in her beat-up old car for a brand-new one. Of course, she quit her after-school job. Her mother decided to go back to school and get a granduate degree in anthropogy, and all of a sudden she started dating college boys.

Before they had so much money, the two of them used to spend time together and get along fine, but now all they do is argue and slam doors. Deep inside Becky hates her new, "improved" life and would give anything to have things the way they used to be. She wants her old friends back and wishes she could wear jeans to school instead of a uniform. But she suffers her stress in silence. She is afraid her mother would think she was ungrateful if she talked about her feelings.

DYSFUNCTIONAL FAMILY RULES

Handed-down codependency, addiction, sexual abuse, physical abuse, verbal or emotional abuse, secrets, and stressful situations all create great internal pressure. If the pressure is not controlled, we may feel as though our families will blow apart like a balloon too full of air. Mothers, fathers, and kids all feel frightened that the explosion will happen at any minute, because people *need* their family.

So, even though they never talk about it or vote on it, families come up with sets of rules to keep from bursting into a million pieces. As long as everybody lives by the rules, the family unit will hang together, even though some members are miserable and their needs are not being met.

It is only logical that the bigger a family's problems and the more internal pressure that builds up, the more rigid the rules become. Eventually, although the rules help the family to survive, they keep us from growing. They're like a balloon made of metal: Nothing can get in, nothing can get out, and there's no room to expand. Living in a metal balloon is like being in prison. What is even worse, when we have lived by these rules long enough, they become part of us. We carry our prison around wherever we go. After a while we start expecting ourselves and everybody else in the world to follow the rules all the time—even though, outside of our dysfunctional families, those rules don't work!

Dysfunctional families rarely talk about their rules. Most of the time we become aware of them only when we break them and are punished. Since the family rules are not posted on the refrigerator or hung over the fireplace, they gain the power of secrets. How can you ever question something that you have to pretend doesn't exist?

If our family did openly talk about the dysfunctional family rules, they would sound something like this:

This family is a closed system. We keep to ourselves and solve our own problems. We don't need any help. You're either for us or against us, and if you make close friends outside of this family or act differently from us, you are not one of us. Other people don't understand us. They might hurt us or take advantage of us. They're all wrong, and we're right. It's us against the world.

Don't talk. Don't even dare to share the secrets of our family with outsiders. And don't talk about them with us either. We *don't* want to hear about it! You'll be a lot happier if you just pretend we don't have any problems. And remember to smile—we wouldn't want anybody to know you're not the happiest, best-adjusted kid in the world.

Don't feel. If it bothers you to keep your feelings inside, then don't feel them. Nobody in our family has ever felt any negative emotions, and nobody ever will. Anger and sadness and pain are signs of weakness. Don't worry about being confused by all this. We have some official family feelings, and we'll tell you what emotions are okay to experience. If you start paying attention to your own feelings, you'll act weird and we won't like it. If you love us, you'll be numb.

Don't Trust. Other people are no good. Everybody breaks promises the way we do. Hey, it's human nature. What can you expect? You had better stop trusting your own perceptions, too. Dad's not drunk; he just has flu. That wasn't an argument you heard; it was the radio. Maybe you should have your hearing checked. Or maybe you're crazy!

We'll love you only if you earn it.   Just being yourself isn't going to cut it. You have to work at gaining our affection, and work hard. Nothing comes without a price, not even love. Do exactly what we tell you to do, and follow all these rules. If you do and you're lucky, we might appreciate you. If you start acting like yourself and thinking for yourself, though, we may pretend you don't exist or even disown you. You know that would be very hard on you because in this family we are the ones who determine your value as a human being. Without us you are nothing.

Shame on you! Really, you ought to be ashamed of yourself. It is nothing you did or can change, it's who you are. Other people make mistakes, but you *are* a mistake. When we pay attention to you and give you affection, we do it out of the goodness of our hearts. You don't deserve that kind of treatment. Sometimes we wonder if you're really a member of this family; you're so different from the way we want you to be. Are you sure you aren't a genetic mutation?

Take care of us. We can't take care of ourselves emotionally, so you must ignore your own needs and meet ours instead. You can start by making us feel better about ourselves. We want to feel important, and we want to feel loved. It would help if you made us the center of your life and forgot about yourself. Thinking about your own needs and trying to meet them is just plain selfish. We expect you to do all the chores around the house and take responsibility for your brothers and sisters, too. We'd like to, you know, but we're so caught up in our problems or addictions that we don't have the time. And don't complain—after all we've done for you, you owe it to us.

Codependent rules may help a dysfunctional family survive as a unit and look good to the outside world. They don't help individual members to thrive, to grow, or to be the people they were meant to be. In truth, they do the opposite. It's no wonder that many of us who grew up in families like these often think that life is terribly unfair and wonder why we were born.

Those sad and angry feelings are very powerful, but we can work past them. The fact that your parents did not meet your needs as you were growing up and that they live by damaging rules now does not doom you to codependency for life. Once you understand where you learned your codependency, you can start making some of your own rules—healthy, growth-promoting rules—and meeting your own needs. It's about time!

CHAPTER ◇ 4

Connecting with the
Kid Inside

Everyone, no matter what their age, has an inner child living inside. Another name for that little kid is our true or authentic self. It is the part of us that is most ourselves. This idea is very hard for some codependent teenagers to believe.

Kevin's parents have meetings after work until seven or eight at night, so after school he has to go right home to take care of his younger brothers and sister. He has been baby-sitting them for as long as he can remember, that and cleaning the house and doing the laundry. Despite his responsibilities around the house, he gets his homework in on time and is on the debate team at school. Kevin certainly doesn't feel as if there's a teenager inside of him, let alone an inner child. Some days feels as if he's forty years old.

Since Maria was in elementary school, teachers have commented on how mature she was for her age.

Maybe part of that had to do with having an alcoholic mother. Not only has Maria had to take care of herself, but she has been pushed into caretaking her mother. Once in ninth grade she had to call the paramedics when her mother, who had been drinking all day, took an overdose of pills. Often since then she has stayed up all night talking to her mother, trying to persuade her that she needs to clean up her act. Maria feels like a crisis counselor; she has never had time to be a carefree kid.

For years boys have thought Cassie was old for her age. Her figure developed early, and using lots of makeup helped. She likes wearing black dresses and high heels because it makes her feel sophisticated, and she likes all the male attention her wardrobe brings her. She sure didn't get any from her father, who abandoned the family when she was five. She has never heard from him, but that's okay; her many boyfriends cheer her up. An inner child is the last thing Cassie wants. Boys don't pay attention to little girls.

Kevin, Maria, and Cassie may deny their inner child, but they have one just the same. You may not feel as though you have an inner child either, especially if people are always telling you:

> "You're so responsible!"
> "Did you say you were twenty-six?"
> "You act a lot older than other kids your age."
> "I couldn't possibly handle a schedule like yours."
> "I've never seen anybody as organized as you are."

When we codependents hear comments like those, we feel good about ourselves. After all, we're used to taking care of other people, and caretakers are responsible people. It's nice to know that the people important to us notice how mature we are and appreciate us for it. We know we must be doing something right. We act so much like adults that we think there is no way *we* could have an inner child.

But we do, just like everybody else in the world. Because we got attention and praise from our families for acting older than our age, we started pretending to be adults when we were very young. Our parents may have seemed to love us more if we acted as though we preferred to do the dishes than go out to play. Our parents were nicer to us, too, if we shrugged and said, "It doesn't matter," when our younger siblings broke our toys, instead of crying or yelling as we wanted to do. When our parents argued, we tried to keep peace in the family, sometimes acting more like adults than they did. We may have provided emotional comfort for a stressed-out parent who needed it often, or we may have been almost totally responsible for taking care of the house.

Even in the best of circumstances, raising children is not easy. Babies and toddlers cry and wet their pants, they get hungry and cry some more, they break things and get things dirty, they need constant attention. Even parents in healthy families sometimes come close to tearing their hair out because little kids are so demanding of time, attention, and unconditional love. Emotionally healthy parents know that kids are a big responsibility. They know that kids have many needs and that it's their job to meet them.

Dysfunctional parents were not sure what they were getting into when they had us. They underestimated our needs. But there we were with all those needs demanding to be met, and often our parents didn't know what to do with us. Even though they may be more at ease as parents now that we're almost grown, back when we were little we missed out on some very important things.

The old saying, "Kids will be kids," does not hold true in dysfunctional families. There kids can't be kids, not if we are to earn our parents' love and positive attention. When we figure out that expressing our needs will bring on a scolding or that our parents will ignore us, we learn to act a lot older than we really are, like little adults.

Appearances can be deceiving. Because our parents could not meet our emotional, and maybe even our physical, needs, the child inside never got a chance to develop. It got stuck at the stage where its needs were ignored. The more we grow physically and the more we take on teenage roles, the wider the split grows between how we act on the outside and our inner child.

Just as being a parent is not easy, being a little kid isn't easy either. Some of the very important lessons we need to learn as we're growing up are to:

- trust the people who take care of us;
- explore the world around us;
- find ways to meet our needs;
- express ourselves;
- know we are individuals;
- feel good about ourselves.

When we are born into a troubled family we miss some of those very important lessons. Sometimes when we were babies the people responsible forgot to feed us, or maybe we were rarely picked up and cuddled. It could be that when we were held, the person holding us was tense or angry and we sensed those feelings. Maybe when we cried nobody ever came to see what was wrong. We learned that we couldn't trust and that the world was a scary, hostile place.

Later our parents may have been afraid to let us explore the world around us, so we never got a chance and we became frightened of what was outside of the playpen or crib. Or maybe we were given freedom to explore but were not watched, so we were hurt. Some of us who are codependent today were not raised in a safe environment. We lived with parents who fought, who threw things, or who yelled and hit us.

Others of us were discouraged from learning to meet our own needs because our parents were codependent. Because they needed to be needed, they may have kept us dependent on them. Everything was done for us, or we were isolated by being forbidden to play with other little kids.

Many of us were not allowed to express ourselves. We were told that kids are meant to be seen and not heard. When we cried or laughed too loudly, our parents made sure we were quiet. If we said things our parents didn't want to hear, we were told to shut up. Children raised in dysfunctional families learn to keep their thoughts, their feelings, their opinions, and their needs to themselves.

Most of us had a tough time learning that we were individuals. Our self-worth depended on being part of a family, not being people in our own right. Because we were not treated as human beings separate from our parents and our independence was discouraged, we didn't experience feeling good about ourselves. How we felt about us depended on how our parents felt about us. At a very early age we were codependents who got through life by living on the outside, trying to make others happy and relying on their opinion of us to make us feel like whole people.

Until we have learned the basic lessons of childhood, we can't move on to more advanced lessons such as sharing, handling frustration, and knowing that we can wait to have our needs met. To learn patience, we have to trust that eventually we'll get what we want. If we rarely get what we want, we sometimes become the demanding two-year-old stamping his or her foot and screaming for a glass of juice—NOW! Or on the outside, we may be people pleasers and act as if we've given up on getting our way, but the kid inside is having a fit, and we feel miserable. It's no wonder our moods and attitudes bounce from one extreme to another with lightning speed.

ACKNOWLEDGING OUR INNER CHILD

Even though we may believe our inner child is an enemy, it is an ally. Only by befriending that part of us can we begin to heal from codependency and start figuring out who we really are. Our inner child always knows what it wants and needs and feels. It doesn't know how to pretend to be happy if it's feeling angry or sad. It doesn't say things it doesn't mean to get others to like it. It doesn't know how to lie.

In codependents the little kid part of us is also hurting because it never got the parenting it needed when it needed it most. As we grow up in a family that does not accept us for who we are, instead of accepting our inner child or our true self as a welcome part of us, we see it as dangerous to our survival. The more codependent we become, the more we learn to live on the ouside.

Eventually we may abandon our inner child completely, turning it into an orphan, making it hurt more and feel even lonelier than it did before.

Or we may admit that it's there but fight with it, becoming inner child abusers. Like all children, the invisible kid inside of us wants love and attention. Because our emotional needs were not met, our inner child is confused, hurting, and craving affection. But instead of loving that child and trying to give it what it needs, we try to make it shut up. We yell at it and put it down, we punish it and shame it. In fact, we may do everything in our power to kill it off.

When any child is treated that way, he or she feels rejected, abandoned, scared, and angry. If we're like most codependents, those inner kid reactions make us come down even harder on ourselves than we did in the first place. We may call ourselves names, tell ourselves we're no good, or find ways to punish ourselves for being human. When we fall into the self-punishment trap for having feelings, we're really abusing the inner child, the true self. Rather than allowing ourselves to be whole human beings with all of our emotional parts working together, we fight ourselves. Sometimes those battles can become all-out war—war with no victor.

Your kid inside does not take the emotional and verbal abuse quietly. The more it is ignored or abused, the more it does everything in its power to get your attention and to get its needs met. It may cry and pout, cringe and shudder in terror, or scream in fits of rage. The longer those needs are ignored, the more strongly your inner child fights you. Like little children in the outside world who are ignored or mistreated, your inner child may go overboard when it finally persuades you to give it what it needs or wants.

After all, it might not get another need met for years. Over time your inner child has learned that it can't trust anybody, especially not you.

> Mark was proud of himself because he had lost twenty pounds on his diet—five more pounds to go and he'd be at his goal weight. He had managed to slim down by skipping lunches and eating only salad for dinner. His weight-loss strategy was far from good for his health, but he justified it as deserved punishment for all the times he had stuffed himself on donuts. He had overeaten for years because he felt left out by his super-athletic older brothers. It was stupid to feel that way, he told himself. Then one day on the way home from school he passed the hamburger stand and it seemed as if a voice inside of him was screaming, "Feed me! Feed me!" He couldn't resist. Seven jumbo hamburgers and three big orders of fries later, he was throwing up in the parking lot. Hating himself, Mark resolved to stop eating even salad at dinner and to lose ten more pounds instead of five.

Because Mark did not understand about the inner child and codependency, his behavior made no sense to him. Why would anybody nearly starve himself to lose weight, then eat like a pig, throw up, and go back to a much stricter diet? Even though Mark would be the last person to admit having a kid inside, his inner child was starved for affection. Over the years he did not admit that sad little boy's presence but quieted him by feeding him donuts. When he stopped eating, his inner kid went bonkers and howled to be taken care of. When Mark gave in at the hamburger stand, his inner kid scored more than a few points, but afterward Mark made a promise to get even. He didn't admit that he had a kid inside; he felt, instead, as though he were being controlled by outside forces. He would show them who was boss!

When codependents deny the kid inside, we run around in circles like Mark and never know what is driving us. Our all-or-nothing behavior is self-defeating, but because we can't admit the child part of us, we blame others for our moods and actions. We can go for months calmly tolerating forgetfulness in a boyfriend or girlfriend; then one night the inner kid gets enraged at two minutes' tardiness and we dump him or her. We can listen to our friends' problems for years, giving advice and lending them money until we feel so used, abused, and uncared for that we stop speaking to them for the rest of our lives. We get straight As by studying all night and then lose the battle with our inner child who wants some fun and sleep. So we stop studying, fail our classes, and believe it's because our teachers are unfair. Until we can connect with the kid inside, we are not really connected to ourselves, so we can't change our either/or actions on a long-term basis. And until we are connected to ourselves, it is impossible for us to connect with other people in a meaningful way.

RECONNECTING WITH THE KID INSIDE

Why, you may wonder, would a teenager well along the path to adulthood want to spend time getting acquainted with some little-bitty inner baby? There must be an easier way! The answer is simple. If you want to heal from codependency, there is no alternative. You cannot have your inner child surgically removed, and you already know that ignoring your true self, yelling at it, or punishing it doesn't work in the long run. The more you ignore, yell, or punish, the more hurt and angry the kid becomes until it controls nearly every move you make—even though that control is done behind the scenes, much like the way the Wizard made things happen in Oz.

You may also be reluctant to meet the kid inside because, from what we have said so far, that inner kid sounds completely depressing or a total brat. It is true that your inner child may feel sad, hurt, or angry. (After all, your little kid grew up in a dysfunctional family!) On the other hand, the child inside can be a positive part of us, too. It is the part that tells jokes and laughs at them, the part that loves music and bright colors, the part that delights in trying new things. Your inner child is:

- full of fun
- joyful
- loving
- a risk-taker
- spontaneous
- creative.

Once you have decided to make friends with your inner child, doing it isn't quite as simple as sitting down and saying, "Okay, you can come out now." That little kid may be a lot of things, but it isn't stupid. It has been in hiding for years because that is where you wanted it to be. Why should your inner child trust you all of a sudden? You haven't trusted it or even listened to it. Maybe this is all a trick, and you're just coaxing it out in the open so you can yell at it some more.

At the start, getting to know your inner child is like playing hide and seek. It takes patience, but it can also be a lot of fun. There are many simple things you can do to help the befriending process along.

MAKING FRIENDS WITH THE KID INSIDE

- Look through the family photo album and find pictures of you as a little kid. Take some time alone to think back to how you felt at that age, to what you looked like and what you liked to do.
- Close your eyes and picture yourself as a little kid. Imagine you're having a conversation with that child and are reassuring him or her that it's okay to come out. You might want to say:

> "I'd like to get to know you."
> "It's safe; I'll protect you."
> "I love you."

- On the first line of a sheet of notebook paper write, "I remember. . .", then finish the sentence. On the next line write, "And I remember. . .," then finish the sentence. Write quickly, and don't stop until you reach the end of the page.
- Still stuck? Draw a picture of what your kid inside would look like (*if* you had one) with crayons. Now write down what you imagine your inner kid would be like.
- Write a letter to your inner child.
- Have your inner child write an answer to that letter.

Once you are acquainted with your inner child and have earned its trust, you can start a working relationship. This time, instead of: The Inner Child Abuser vs. The Brat, you have a chance to form a healthy relationship with your authentic self. Because your kid inside did not have all of its developmental needs met, the two of you are not quite ready for an absolutely equal partnership. First your inner child needs to do a little growing up. While you are recovering from codependency, your inner kid or your true self still needs to be parented. And this time it's up to *you* to be loving parent.

One of the most important things loving parents do is to acknowledge their children's presence by listening to them. Hearing the voice of your inner child takes practice, especially when you're used to shutting it out. You can start listening by setting aside some quiet time every day, time when you are alone and can sit for a few minutes to get in touch with your inner kid.

If quiet time doesn't work, you might try writing a dialog with your inner child, asking it what it wants and needs, asking how you can help it to heal and to feel better about itself. Many codependents have found that this technique works best when they use the hand they usually write with to record their questions and the hand they don't usually write with to record their inner kid's answers. Your dialog might turn out something like Karen's:

Karen: Why are you always so sad?
Inner Kid: Because you won't let me talk!
Karen: That's because you say dumb stuff.
Inner Kid: No, I don't. I say stuff that can help you.
Karen: Like what?
Inner Kid: Like lighten up on yourself.

In addition to listening, loving parents set limits. They do not allow their children to stay up all night, live on candy bars, or go around hitting people. Learning to live with positive and fair rules is a good thing. When we set limits on the little kid inside of us, we are learning self-discipline. The child inside needs to know that while it's okay to feel, it is not always okay to act on those feelings, especially if it means harming other people or ourselves.

If we cannot set reasonable limits on our inner kid or we are frightened by what our inner child is feeling, it's a good idea to talk to a teacher or a counselor. When Nat started working with his inner child, he was shocked to find out that it was boiling with anger. He had always prided himself on being a cool and casual person who didn't let anything get to him, not even his mother's addiction to tranquilizers. Now he didn't feel like smiling and saying, "Hi," to friends in the hall—he wanted to shout at them. He began blowing up at Mrs. Garvey, his chemistry teacher, and he broke up with his girlfriend. For a while he tried running and lifting weights to get rid of his inner kid's negative energy, but that didn't work and he began to worry that he might be going crazy. Finally, he talked to a counselor at school and found out that her office was a safe place to let off steam. Because she knew about codependency, she could work with Nat to help him set some workable rules for his inner kid.

Setting rules and listening are only part of the reparenting we can do for our inner child. You can spend time with the kid inside and do nice things for it. Some of those things might be:

- Really listening the next time you get a compliment.
- Wearing a color that makes you look super.
- Laughing.
- Seeing a movie you want to see.
- Asking a friend for a hug.
- Going out for dinner.

How many more can you think of?
How many more can your inner child think of?

CHAPTER 5

Beating the
Shame Game

As soon as Mr. Grant started handing back the algebra tests, Robert got a sinking feeling in the pit of his stomach. He knew he had not done very well. No matter how hard he tried, he just couldn't figure out binomial equations. Finally, there it was: a huge F written in bright red marking pen. The grade was so big it covered the whole first page. The entire class laughed as Mr. Grant laid the test with a flourish on Robert's desk. "Some students have tapioca pudding for brains," the teacher said with a sneer. Robert's classmates laughed louder. "Ignorance can be corrected with education, but stupidity. . ." Mr. Grant raised his eyebrows, shrugged his shoulders, and walked to the board to begin his lecture for the day.

Robert could feel his face growing so hot that it seemed as red as the F on the test in front of him. He wanted to run out the door, but that would make the kids *really* tease him. Instead he sat quietly, trying to be invisible and hoping against hope that the floor would open and swallow him whole. It wasn't as if he didn't know he was stupid. His father had been telling him so for years, and Dad was probably right. Still, it was humiliating to have his teacher and the whole class make fun of him. He was so ashamed he wished he could resign from the human race.

All teenagers feel ashamed of themselves at one time or another, especially when their weaknesses are exposed in front of people they want to like them. Codependent teenagers live with shame constantly. Our sinking feelings of humiliation grow out of our belief that something is very wrong with who we are. As codependents we're fairly sure we were born defective, and once other people find out how horrible we are inside, they won't want to have anything to do with us.

When a friend, a teacher, or a parent abuses us emotionally, instead of getting angry we believe we deserve that cruel treatment. After all, the Mr. Grants of the world are not telling us anything we didn't know already. Our families made it clear to us at a very young age that we were not good enough, and no matter how hard we tried, there wasn't a thing we could do to change it. Our shame robs us of our dignity and disconnects us from the human race.

UNDERSTANDING SHAME

Before we can start freeing ourselves from our burden of shame, we need to learn exactly what it is and why we codependents carry it around with us all the time. We may confuse shame with guilt in our minds. Although the two are related, they are not the same emotion. We feel guilt when our actions are out of line, and that emotion in small amounts can be a good thing because it helps us to change our ways. If we feel guilty about not answering test questions correctly, we can ask for help even if that means getting a tutor. If we feel a stab of guilt from overeating, we can go on a diet. Guilt is the emotion that moves us to say we're sorry when we make a hurtful remark to a friend, forget something important, or even do something like stealing or lying.

Shame is different because it is not about what we do but who we *are*. If we are ashamed because we think we were born without brains, we are stuck with that unhappy fact, certain that we can do nothing to make our lives better. If we are ashamed about being awful people who are without self-discipline, we don't go on a diet when we put on extra pounds; we eat whole bags of cookies to ease our emotional pain. People who are filled with shame do not apologize just for doing or saying things that hurt other people, they apologize for being alive.

We feel guilty when we believe we made a mistake; we feel shame when we believe we *are* a mistake. If we grow up in a family where we learn to be ashamed of who we are, where we feel unworthy and unlovable, we may be so used to thinking we're not good enough that we forget there are other ways to feel. It's like living with a sore tooth for years before going to the dentist to get it fixed. Even though we are in constant pain, we push that sensation below our awareness. Just because we pretend everything is fine doesn't mean it is.

Once the emotional pain of shame becomes an everyday fact of life, we hand that uncomfortable feeling to our inner child to carry. We may be able to fool ourselves for a time, but we can never completely block out our feelings that we are not worthy of love or are not as good as other people. The hurt little kid inside of us feels them for us, and it makes decisions for us based on that shame. When we feel like crying for no reason or suddenly feel frightened and want to run away but don't know why, chances are that our shamed little kid inside is crying out for help.

Since we have learned to ignore our feelings in order to survive in our families, codependents have a hard time knowing when we are feeling shame. Instead of calling our shame by the right name, which gives us the power to do something about it, we may call it craziness or stupidity or weakness. And that gives us even more to feel ashamed about.

How can you tell when you're feeling shame? You're having a shame attack when you:

- Hang out with people who constantly put you down, and you *believe* them.
- Feel physically smaller than you are or feel like a bad little kid.
- Get a burning red face and wish you could disappear. (That wanting-to-vanish feeling stays with you for hours or even days.)
- Feel worse and worse about yourself.
- Feel helpless, as if there's nothing you can do to change.
- Can't look other people in the eyes.
- Find yourself "numbing out" emotionally so that you feel wooden or like a robot.
- Get tongue-tied; either your mind goes blank, or the words just won't come out.
- Feel your energy level dropping to the point at which you're paralyzed.

- Believe that you deserve it when people call you names or say hurtful things to you.
- Start calling yourself names and putting yourself down, treating yourself worse than others have been treating you.
- Believe that you're no good and that nothing you ever do, or will do, is good enough.
- Wish you had never been born.

YOU OUGHT TO BE ASHAMED OF YOURSELF!

Even though you may not be able to remember a time when you didn't feel ashamed, shame is not an emotion that any of us are born with. Psychologists have found that kids don't start being ashamed of themselves until they are about a year and a half old. That is long after babies discover pleasure, surprise, disgust, sadness, fear, joy, anger, and love. Before we can experience shame, we have to gain the self-awareness that we are separate from our parents or caretakers and that we depend on them to feed us and watch us because they love us. Once we get the idea that we could be abandoned, we become very upset when we sense that love might be taken away from us. After all, if nobody had cared about us enough to take care of us, we would have died.

Most little kids first feel shame when they do something that upsets their parents. When they see parents' anger, they know that they could be abandoned. We learned when we were very young that if we took our clothes off in the grocery store or yelled swear words when company came, our parents would be furious. Because we were afraid they wouldn't love us, we kept our clothes on and our mouths shut.

Kids who are raised in healthy families feel shame, but only briefly. Their parents get angry at them, but that anger doesn't last long. They don't rage at their kids or threaten to get rid of them forever. They *do* hug their children and make up with them after they have scolded or punished them. Because the strained emotional bond with their parents is mended quickly, kids in healthy families learn that *they* were not bad; it was their actions. They can be forgiven. What a relief!

Dysfunctional families are a different story. Forgiveness is rare in these homes. Little kids may live in terror that they'll be kicked out of the house and that their parents will hate them forever. When they do things that make their parents angry, they're told they are terrible kids and that something is wrong with them. Sometimes they don't even do anything wrong but are just acting their age, and they're still called bad. Their emotional bond with their parents is broken and may not be repaired for days or weeks or months, so their feelings of shame and disconnectedness are overwhelming.

When Shari was four, her mother gave her a set of tiny doll dishes that had belonged to her grandmother. She loved the fragile little cups and saucers and tried to be careful, but she broke several of them. When her mother saw the pieces of china she went into a fury and accused her daughter of smashing the teacups on purpose. "You hate me," shrieked Shari's mother through her tears. "You're an ungrateful, no-good daughter. I wish you'd never been born." Instead of admitting her own poor judgment in giving antiques to a preschooler, she blamed Shari for being a typical four-year-old—something the little girl could not help or change. Neither could she help being born. Instead of becoming a useful part of her conscience, Shari's shame followed her over the years and kept her from ever accepting presents with joy, from letting herself have pretty things, and even from making friends.

All parents make occasional shaming statements to their kids. Parents are human beings, and they make mistakes. In healthy families parents know they've made a mistake and admit it to their children. Healthy parents punish their kids, but they also show love for them soon afterward. In dysfunctional families, parents *often* shame their kids into minding. Some typical things a kid growing up in a dysfunctional family may hear are:

"You're a jerk, just like your father."
"I wish you'd never been born."
"How can you do this to me!"
"You're no good."
"You never do anything right."
"You're stupid."
"You're crazy."
"You're never going to find a man to love you."
"You're not part of this family!"
"What's wrong with you?"

Kid don't have to hear statements like these very often to be convinced that they're no good. They think they don't deserve to loved, to be cared for, or even to be alive. They know they have to work extra hard to be perfect on the outside so they'll be accepted. And they're afraid to show their true selves to anyone. To let other people, even their parents, see them as they really are is too great a risk.

Parents do not necessarily shame their children because they don't love them. Some parents who say cruel things to their kids grew up in families where *they* were shamed. They may think that shaming kids is the proper way to raise them. Even when they know that their angry words and threats hurt their children, these parents often don't know how else to make their children behave.

In some families feeling good about yourself is confused with arrogance and pride, so kids are shamed for having self-esteem. In fact, self-esteem may even be considered sinful. Parents work so hard to teach their kids to respect other people and to be humble that they go overboard. They may never praise their sons and daughters but criticize them often because they think it's good for them. In these families self-hatred becomes a virtue.

Other parents tease their children to the point of tears. Marilyn's father made a big joke out of her developing figure, and soon her older brothers joined in the "fun." When she told them to stop it, they said she was too sensitive. It got so bad that she hated to go home after school, and sitting at the dinner table was torture. When the men in the family chipped in to buy her an outrageously huge bra for her thirteenth birthday and called her a cow, she cried for days. Her mother told her not to get upset, that if they didn't love her they wouldn't tease her. That made her feel worse because now she was ashamed of her reaction to the teasing. She couldn't stop her transformation into a woman, but she was humiliated about her body and did her best to hide it by wearing baggy sweaters even in the summer.

Words are not the only things that can cause us to feel shame. When we are neglected either physically or emotionally as children, we tend to blame ourselves for the neglect. It doesn't matter whether our parents are neglecting us on purpose or because of a crisis we have nothing to do with, such as a death in the family or a sibling born with a birth defect. We believe that if we were better kids our parents would buy food for us or spend time with us.

Sometimes we blame ourselves not only for the neglect, but for the problem that caused it, such as alcoholism or divorce. If we were better looking or kinder or smarter, maybe our parent wouldn't drink so much. Maybe Mom and Dad would have stayed married. We may blame ourselves so much for family problems that we believe the whole family would be happy today if we had not been born.

When we live in families that have problems easily seen by outsiders, we can start to feel even more shame as we grow up. The older we get, the more aware we are of what the neighbors think and of what our friends think. We view our families as a reflection of the kind of persons we are, and we may be too ashamed to bring friends home or to make friends in the first place.

Often codependent teenagers carry a big burden of shame because they were physically or sexually abused. We mistakenly think that we made a parent hit us or molest us, not necessarily because of something we said or did, but because of who we are. Even though we may know in our minds that what happened to us wasn't our fault, in our hearts we are sure that something is so wrong with us that we triggered and deserved the abuse.

Both family violence and incest are family secrets, events we are told not to talk about within the family or with other people. Many families have a secret that is not as damaging to children as battering or sexual abuse. Maybe a grandparent committed suicide or an aunt or uncle was sent to jail long ago. Parents often keep these family skeletons from their kids because they think the truth would hurt them. The opposite is true—secrets hurt!

When anything is a secret, it tends to make us feel even more shame, even when we don't know what the secret is. We grow up feeling that something is wrong with our family; that it is not as good as other families; that it is different and somehow bad. We may have no idea what we are ashamed of, but because we are part of the family, we share the shame.

Shame is often like a disease that runs in families, that is passed from parents to children. Because feeling unworthy and unlovable hurts so much, people who suffer from those damaging beliefs will do anything to get rid of them. Unless they understand what they feel and why they feel it, they pass their shame to others without thinking. When we say and do things that make other people feel bad about themselves, for a few minutes at least we can feel that we are better than them. Even though we may not be good enough, at least we're not as terrible as the person we just insulted or hurt.

Much of the shame we carry inside today really belongs to others. Some may come from parents who were severely punished when they laughed or played or made a normal amount of noise for kids their age. To ease their shameful feelings, they punished us too severely. Some may come from parents who were made to feel bad about themselves when their parents hit them, kicked them, or called them names. For a minute or two their pain went away when they hit us, kicked us, or called us names. Or maybe our parents were sexually abused, neglected, or lived with an alcoholic parent. Even though they may not have molested us, neglected us, or become alcoholic, chances are they gave us some of their shame about their own childhood.

Shame says more about the person who is doing the shaming than about the person being shamed. When we are little kids, however, we have no way of understanding that, no way of saying, "Hey, Mom and Dad, that's your shame and I'm not going to accept it as my own no matter what you say or do to me."

Once words or events convince us that we are not worthy of love, we believe that we must work very hard to hide our true selves. Our shame and the reason for it become a secret, sometimes even to us. We develop a false self and go through life acting a role rather than living out who we are. Being ourselves just isn't good enough. We're afraid that if we don't pretend to be perfect, people will reject us. When trying to be perfect doesn't work, we may hide from others, running away from relationships and spending much of our time alone. We're ashamed and ashamed of being ashamed. Even when we're with other people, we feel cut off from them, disconnected, different.

BEATING THE SHAME GAME

The first step in overcoming our feelings of being unworthy and unlovable is to recognize when we're feeling shame instead of hiding our misery from the world and ourselves. Until we can admit feeling ashamed, we are helpless. When we stuff that emotion inside and give it to our inner child, it doesn't go away. Instead it gets worse.

Try carrying a small notebook or a piece of paper with you for a few days. Go back over the list of shame symptoms at the beginning of this chapter and write down the ones you feel when you have a shame attack. What was said or done that triggered the attack? Does anything about that time remind you of how you felt when you were younger? Are you reminded of anything that *happened* to you when you were younger? How long did your feelings of shame last this time? What did you say or do? What did you wish you had said or done?

Don't be upset with yourself if it takes you a while to know when you're feeling shame. Because we codependents are out of touch with our feelings, it can take us hours or even days to figure out the cause of our emotional discomfort. With practice you will be able to detect shame almost as soon as it strikes, or at least before you get caught in a shame spiral, a downward cycle of self-criticism and self-hatred.

Even when other people *don't* say or do things that strike shame into our hearts, codependents are great experts at shaming themselves. All it takes is some teasing or a critical remark and our self-shaming tapes click on. They sound something like this: "I'm just no good...I never do anything right...And I look funny too...I've never had any friends and I never will...I'm just a boring person...Stupid too...I shouldn't have been born...I'm a mistake...I'm just no good."

We may not be able to control how other people treat us, but we can control how we treat ourselves. When you catch yourself overreacting by starting to play your self-shaming tapes, STOP! Take a few deep breaths and play another tape in your mind, one like: "I'm basically a good person...Sure I made a mistake, but everybody makes mistakes...I'm only human...I accept the way I look...Even if I don't have friends right now, I will someday...After all, I'm interesting and bright...I'm glad I was born...I'm a good person!"

Some codependents get stuck at this point because they can't think of a single good thing to say about themselves. If you're having that problem, do your homework. Make a list of good points about yourself so you can carry it with you and read it before you begin beating yourself up emotionally. If you still can't think of anything nice about you, try to remember all the compliments you've ever received and write those down. Or ask a friend or relative who loves you, "Hey, just what is it you see in me?" Instead of arguing with them when they say nice stuff, write those compliments down!

We need to take a long, hard look at the people we choose to be around. Even though we may not be able to avoid negative folks who delight in cutting us down to size, we can try to cut down our contact with them. We can also make an extra effort to be good to ourselves when we know we have to be around a blamer or a shamer, so that we don't take on their shame as our own.

Since we learned to feel shame in our early relationships with people who rejected us, we need to work toward healthy relationships with people who will accept us. If we're not comfortable talking with kids our age, we can form a friendship with a teacher, a school counselor, or a youth worker—someone we trust enough to be ourselves around, someone who will listen to us. Because shame grows in secrecy and isolation, its cure lies in reconnecting ourselves with the human race one small step at a time.

Some codependent teens who start exploring their feelings of shame have frightening memories pop up. Kids who have been sexually molested or beaten often repress or forget those events, pushing them to the back of their minds because they can't deal with the emotional or physical pain at the time. When those painful memories resurface, it can feel like a terrible nightmare—especially when you had no idea you had been a victim of battering or sexual abuse.

As you read this book, if you find your memories or feelings are too much to cope with alone, take a break and talk to a counselor. Sharing your secret with someone who is professionally trained to listen and who understands can help take away your shame. Everybody needs a little help sometimes, especially codependents who have gone through life convinced that they should be able to do everything by themselves.

Although learning to love and accept ourselves does not happen overnight (and codependents do want *everything* to happen overnight), we can slowly and deliberately replace negative and shaming thoughts about ourselves with a more positive point of view. As we make this self-image overhaul, our inner child begins to heal and we don't feel quite so crushed when others occasionally make fun of us or reject us. We start to like and accept ourselves as we really are and stop giving other people's opinions power over our lives.

After all, since you are the best friend you're ever going to have throughout your life, it makes perfect sense to treat yourself with kindness and respect.

CHAPTER ◇ 6

Dealing with
Feelings

Shame is not the only emotion we codependents carry around inside of us, even though it may sometimes seem that way, especially once we begin to notice our emotions. That is because most of us, when we bury our feelings, hide them under a big pile of shaming self-hatred. When we first start trying to discover the feelings we have stuffed away, we may encounter so much shame that it discourages us. If that happens and we feel like giving up, we need to hang in there until we get past the shame and uncover our true selves. Before we can really heal, we need to find and feel *all* of our feelings. Beneath them lie the joy and peace in our inner core of being.

Why are we codependents so ashamed of having feelings? When we were little kids and we expressed an emotion forbidden in our families, whether it was fear or joy or anger or love, chances are we were made fun of or punished. Feelings are not allowed in dysfunctional families, sometimes not even physical feelings, because there is simply no room for them. All the problems and pressures in dysfunctional families make feelings forbidden.

For as long as Bill, now a high school senior, can remember, his mother and father taught him that men are not supposed to show pain. Even when he was a toddler and learning to walk, if he fell down his father yelled at him to stop crying like a sissy. Not too much later he began being spanked—something to *really* cry about—when he hurt himself playing. By the time his mother died two years ago he didn't cry or feel much of anything. Now he is so good at feeling no pain that last month when he fractured his leg after falling off his motorcycle, he limped around for two days before going to the doctor.

Kelly's family prides themselves on how well they all get along. Part of the reason they seem so calm on the surface could be that nobody really talks to anybody else, at least not about important things. Years ago when Kelly disagreed with her folks as all kids do, her mother would cry. "If you loved me, you wouldn't be such a hateful child," she would say when her daughter wanted to wear a blue sweater instead of a red one or refused to eat her vegetables. Now that Kelly is a teenager, everybody remarks on how she never gets mad. Nobody notices that she isn't happy, either.

Jeff and his sister, Ellen, grew up with parents who felt uncomfortable touching their kids. Neither one of them can remember sitting on a parent's lap or being hugged. When they were much younger they tried to show affection for their folks, but they were roughly pushed away. Even saying, "I love you," was discouraged as being mushy. Today when Jeff and Ellen begin to feel a desire to make friends with their high school classmates, they are confused and frightened. Both of them emotionally push people away with sarcasm and stuck-up attitudes. They avoid friendships at all costs because they believe something is shamefully wrong with wanting to be close to other people.

When kids like Bill, Kelly, Jeff, and Ellen are teased, humiliated, or punished for having feelings, a deep sense of shame sticks to those outlawed emotions like glue. Whether we were scolded for getting angry, made to feel guilty for being afraid, or punished for acting too happy, we learned early that to feel is shameful. Something is wrong with us not only for expressing our feelings, but for having them in the first place. We believe that our emotions make us defective. Soon whenever we even start to feel angry, scared, happy, or whatever emotion was banned in our families, our shame instantly stops us from experiencing that feeling. Now all we feel is bad about ourselves. We believe we must be terrible people, but because we seldom remember being shamed as little kids, we don't know what is wrong with us.

Finally we run from our shame by making ourselves feel numb. If we have no feelings, it's impossible for our feelings to be hurt, we think. "Who needs feelings?" we tell ourselves. "Feelings just get me into trouble. It's safer not to feel." One major problem with that philosophy of life is that by cutting ourselves off from our emotions to avoid feeling any pain, hurt, or shame, we don't allow ourselves to feel joy or tenderness or affection either.

Our feelings are a normal part of being human. No

matter how hard we try to avoid them, we have them all our lives. And all feelings—even the negative ones—help us to make wise choices about how to live. If we find ourselves always being angry or sad when we're around certain people, we can choose not to be friends with them. If we feel happy in the presence of other people, we can choose to spend more time with them. If history frustrates us, but we feel joy when we do chemistry experiments, we decide to major in chemistry in college, even though our parents say becoming a history teacher is the right career choice for us.

STUFFING FEELINGS

Codependent teenagers have a hard time making their feelings work for them because they have told themselves they don't feel a thing so often that they believe it. Much of the time we are totally out of touch with our feelings. When emotions start oozing toward the surface, we are so ashamed and afraid of them that we stuff them deeper. And then we are paralyzed when it comes to making conscious choices. Instead of basing our decisions on our own feelings and from our own hearts, we make our choices based on what other people are feeling or might feel.

If Grandpa says, "Go to college and be a historian," that's what we do because it would be a shame to hurt his feelings or disappoint him. We ignore our own feelings, stuffing them deeper inside. If our best friend fixes us up on a double date with "somebody we should really like," we don't stop to ask ourselves whether we're attracted to the person. We go and spend the evening trying to like our date in order to please our friend. If Aunt Matilda, who promised to buy us a car for our sixteenth birthday, gives us a pair of orange and purple socks instead, we can't feel disappointed. Only an ungrateful, bad, terrible person would feel that way. Not us! We write Aunt Matilda a three-page letter thanking her for the socks, then wear them to school and wonder why we have the blahs.

Even though we may be able to fool ourselves into believing that we love history, are impressed by our blind date, or were dying for a pair of orange and purple socks—we can't fool our inner child or true self. It still feels extremely angry or sad or betrayed, no matter how we act on the outside. Every time we stuff our emotions, we give that little kid inside a bigger burden to carry, a suffocating burden.

Since we pay no attention to how our inner child feels or to what is in our hearts, those emotions stay bottled up for days, weeks, months, or sometimes years. Instead of being the creative, spontaneous little kid our inner child was intended to be, it is buried beneath the feelings we refuse to feel. That kind of treatment is enough to make anybody mad—angry at us and angry at the world.

Eventually the pressure becomes too much to contain and we explode emotionally, usually over some incident that most people would consider minor. Grandpa buys us a history book and we stop speaking to him. We break off with our best friend because of an argument over fifteen cents. Next time we see Aunt Matilda we call her a liar to her face. We don't know what got into us, so we feel more ashamed than ever and begin the emotion-stuffing cycle all over again.

When we deny our emotions, we often tell ourselves we're just looking on the bright side. We may even congratulate ourselves for not being upset at the things that bother our friends. We're cool, calm, and collected, we believe. We have a positive attitude toward life. We don't let things get to us. For most of us, though, our positive attitude isn't real. Rather it is an act we have practiced so often that we believe the illusion.

A codependent in the midst of denying her emotions will tell you, "I'm okay," right after she lost her job, failed English, and her cat died. Deep inside she craves comforting, but she can't admit feeling vulnerable even to herself. Ask a codependent if it bothered him when vandals stole the tape player in his car, and he'll say, "Not really; it was no big deal." He'll believe it, too, but inside he's simmering with resentment. Weeks later that resentment is still festering like an infection, so that when his friends make a joke at his expense he gets into a fistfight. Afterward he has no idea why he lost his temper.

The trouble with ignoring our feelings is that even though we can hide from them temporarily, we can't run away from our inner emotional state forever. While we pretend to ourselves and the world that we don't feel a thing, those emotions we deny are churning away inside and turning into resentment or depression. By overcontrolling our emotions on a short-term basis, we sometimes completely lose control in the long run, throwing temper tantrums or getting so down that we feel suicidal.

We also put ourselves through a great deal of day-to-day physical stress. It is not uncommon for codependents to suffer from stomach troubles, backaches, and tension headaches because of the anxiety they endure trying to pretend they don't feel what they feel. When we get keyed up, people may advise us to take it easy. But we can't very well relax until we can let go of our feelings, and that is impossible as long as we maintain that we don't have any. How can we lighten up when we refuse to admit the burden we force our inner child to carry?

FEELINGS STEALING AND MIND READING

Often codependent teenagers know they should be feeling *something* besides the confusion or numbness they usually know. After all, everybody else seems to have feelings, sometimes very pleasant feelings, so it's hard not to be envious. Because we have learned to live through other people, rather than looking inside for our emotional answers, codependents study other people to figure out what we should be feeling. Often that strategy turns into feelings stealing when we consciously pretend that our emotions match those of the people around us.

When Becky is with a group of kids, she sits quietly and checks out how everybody else is feeling. When she is with friends who are angry about the new attendance policy at school, she gets furious about it, too. In English Lit class, where most of the students believe that the new attendance rules are good, Becky agrees with them. In fact, she is filled with school pride and can't understand how her friends could be so childish—until she talks with them again. Then she's upset at the principal and feels that her classmates in English Lit are a bunch of stuck-up snobs.

Most teenagers jump from position to position because they find out who they are by trying on a number of attitudes, feelings, and beliefs to see which fit them best. We also go through times when we want to conform, to be like the people around us. Kids like Becky, however, rarely seem to know their own hearts and minds. They imitate the emotions of those they happen to be with, never stopping to figure out where they stand. They don't merely want to be accepted by one group; they need to be the same as everybody else in the world. After a while codependent feelings stealers begin to feel like a rubber band pulled so far in two directions they think they might snap.

Trying to read other people's minds so that we can know what they're feeling and imitate those emotions begins when we're young. In our dysfunctional families we have to stay on top of others' feelings to protect ourselves. When we don't at least put on a good show of what is expected of us, we can be in big trouble. If Mom is feeling depressed because of Dad's drinking problem, we need to get depressed about it and empathize with her in order to earn her love. To act joyful because of something that happened at school would be disloyal. If Dad is angry at our brother and has stopped speaking to him, we have to work ourselves into the same set of feelings or Dad will hate us, too. To show kindness or compassion to our brother would be seen as betraying Dad.

When we pretend to feel something long enough, we become so used to it that we actually believe the feeling is our own. Instead of acting on our true emotions, we base our decisions on feelings we have taken from others. Smile long enough and you'll think you're happy, even though you are crying inside. By the same token, hang out with depressed and negative people long enough and you'll start to take on their gloom.

Sometimes taking on the feelings of others happens below the level of our awareness. Codependent teens can be so out of touch with their own emotional states that they "catch" the emotions of their friends and family members without knowing it—much as they would catch a cold or the flu. We may try to talk ourselves into believing that we feel empathy or sympathy for others. We convince ourselves that we are intuitive and are getting very close to people, when actually we are confusing their feelings with our own. Since we are not tuned in to our own emotional states we can't tell when others are bringing us down or making us angry. And we can't make a conscious choice to listen or not, to be affected or not, to leave or to stay. In this way, other people's emotions rule our lives.

Sam's friend, Bob, broke up with his steady girlfriend two weeks ago, and all he can talk about is how terrible women are and how they hurt a guy any chance they get. Sam was getting along pretty well with his own girlfriend until he "caught" Bob's attitude. Now he wonders if she is seeing another boy behind his back. His jealousy is not based on anything she has done or even on his own feelings. But it has inspired him to pick fights with her and even to think about breaking up.

When we are not trying to read minds, stealing other people's feelings, or catching them, we may encourage other people to tell us what we are feeling or should be feeling. Usually we find another codependent to fill this role, someone who is so out of touch with his or her own emotions that he or she lives through other people, dominating them with bossiness.

Elana, who began dating later than most of the girls in her class, feels insecure with her new boyfriend. Sometimes she loves him and can't imagine living without him. Other times she's terrified at having a close relationship. Instead of facing her own conflicting feelings and trying to find answers for herself, she asks her best friend for advice. During these conversations. she tells her friend everything her boyfriend said and did on their latest date and quizzes her friend about how she should feel and what she should do. Sometimes it's as though Elana's best friend and her boyfriend are the two people really having a relationship, even though they have never gone out together.

We can be lifelong experts at denying our emotions, but sometimes they still get dangerously close to our aware- ness. When that happens we may tell ourselves that they belong to our friends or family members instead of us. When we experience our feelings through other people, counselors say we are projecting. That's a good word for it, because we are using the people as though they were a blank movie screen and casting our scary emotions onto them. It's as though we were movie projectors. If we feel like lying to other people, we may not be able to admit it to ourselves, so we believe we're surrounded by liars. Every- one we meet is trying to trick us. When we are angry and denying our anger, we think other people are mad at us. Projecting is an effective way to avoid taking responsibility for our own emotions and actions. It is also an effective way to destroy friendships.

"You're angry at me. What did I do to make you mad?" Nancy asked her friend, Janice, at lunch. "You won't talk to me. You're usually so talkative. I know I did something and you hate me. Please tell me what I did." Janice said she had just blown a geometry test and didn't want to discuss it, but Nancy, who had been stuffing envy over her friend's new boyfriend for weeks, persisted. "You're jealous because I get As in geometry. That's what the problem is. If you're going to be so childish, we can't be friends anymore. I can't stand it." Instead of dealing with her own envy, she projected it onto her friend and used it as an excuse to end the relationship.

FEELING AND HEALING

Even though you may be unsure of yourself when you begin, feeling your feelings is not nearly as complicated as stuffing them, mind reading, feelings stealing, or projecting. You already know there are no winners in the emotional games codependents play with themselves and with other people. Even so, when you're used to second-hand emotions, dealing with your own feelings can be a little scary at first.

Before we can admit our feelings we have to figure out just what we are feeling and give a name to it. Many codependents are not sure. It may take us days or weeks to discover that we are angry at a careless remark a friend made or that we have been having a shame attack instead of the flu or mono we had feared. Naming our feelings is the first step in claiming them as our own. You may be feeling:

Confused	Certain
Angry	Affectionate
Afraid	Courageous
Ashamed	Confident
Suspicious	Trusting
Lonely	Involved
Bored	Interested
Hateful	Loving
Resentful	Forgiving

Tense	Calm
Hurt	Comforted
Sad	Happy
Impatient	Patient
Disappointed	Satisfied

See how many other possibilities you can come up with.

Since codependents are used to all-or-nothing thinking, we may believe that our feelings are all good or all bad, all black or all white. We think we can either hate or love a person—there's no middle ground. In reality the middle ground between any of the pairs of emotions above is filled with all kinds of emotions. If you feel angry your emotion can run all the way from mild irritation to blinding fury. When you feel affection it can range from liking a person a little bit to feeling as though you want to spend your life with the person.

Like developing an eye for looking at paintings and seeing all the subtleties and gradations of color and of light and shade, accurately understanding what we feel takes time. It takes practice, too, and in the beginning that means making guesses—and sometimes being wrong. Because you are learning, your guesses may be a little off target and a little late, but they'll become faster and more accurate with time. That's because we always do know what we're feeling deep inside at the inner child or true self level.

Feeling our feelings is mostly a matter of listening to what our inner child is telling us and trusting what we hear. If you are confused or convinced that you don't feel a thing, ask your inner child what it is feeling. Or take some quiet time alone to sit down and imagine what you might be feeling *if* you had a feeling.

Another way to recover your lost feelings is to start

paying attention to how your body reacts in a situation. Does your mouth get dry, or do you start having a stomachache? Do your hands get sweaty or your knees start to shake? Our bodies can provide valuable clues about our feelings.

All this information may be too much to keep track of at once. That's why many people healing from codependency find it useful to keep a journal. Whether they use a spiral notebook, a legal pad, or a fancy diary, writing down what happens and how they react to it helps them. A journal can be a place to store our feelings when we can't deal with them right away, instead of stuffing them. We also have a private place to work with and through our emotions. Journals give us a record of our progress, too. It's nice to look back and see how much we have grown.

Here are some things you can do in your journal:

- Imagine that the emotions you feel are characters or persons. Write down what they look like, how they dress, how they walk and talk. Where and when were they born? What do they like and dislike?
- Write a dialog between you and the emotion you're working with. Ask the feeling questions in writing, and write down what the feeling answers.
- If you can't find the words, draw a picture of how you're feeling or make a collage by cutting bits of pictures out of magazines and gluing them on the page, then writing about them.

When we allow ourselves to name, claim, and fully experience our feelings, the negative ones usually don't last very long. Even if we feel hurt or sad or angry, those emotions eventually flow through us and leave room for feelings of happiness and inner calm. It is when we deny them that our feelings freeze up as solidly as a river in winter. Only when we admit all our feelings and accept them as a part of who we are, can we begin to thaw and let go of them.

Some people who practice martial arts see it another way. They call that tactic embracing the tiger. When we can gather the courage to hug our tigerish and frightening feelings, often they turn out to be pussycats instead of the wild and dangerous threats our denial made them out to be. They may even go away and leave us in peace, but before they will stop bothering us they need a good-bye hug.

Even though our feelings are not necessarily a matter of choice, we can decide how to deal with them. It is our minds chattering away with resentment that make our feelings seem bigger and scarier than they really are. When we start blowing things out of proportion, we can stop the negative things we are saying to ourselves and say positive things instead.

Feelings are not the same as actions. Whether we are excited or scared or angry or affectionate, it is always our choice whether or not to act on our feelings. We can also always choose *how* to act on our feelings. The decision is up to us.

When our feelings make us stressed out, we can take a time-out from them by learning to relax. Deep breaths work sometimes. At other times we may need to take a walk or do some aerobics. Physical exercise usually makes us feel calmer and gives us the emotional space to put our feelings into perspective.

Finally, we need to remember that feelings provide us with gifts. The positive side effects of love and joy and trust are obvious. But emotions such as anger and sadness have their up side, too. Anger is something many of us need to feel before we decide to change. If we did not feel sadness or grief over our losses, we couldn't heal from them. Our emotions—all of them—are just what we need to be happy, healthy human beings.

CHAPTER 7

Speaking Out

Once we come to terms with our emotions, the next task we face in healing from our codependency is learning how to communicate those feelings to other people. Unfortunately, most of us grew up in dysfunctional families that had a "Don't Talk" rule. Some of us were told that children were meant to be seen and not heard, so we learned to be silent much of the time. Others were raised in families where people talked *all* the time. They jabbered away constantly but did not discuss important issues or say anything that revealed feelings. Emotions were not discussed—ever.

Some of us discovered that our parents or older siblings put us down whenever we said something. We found that expressing ourselves honestly and openly meant risking shame, so we learned to lie about how we felt. It is not surprising that today many of us are ashamed to say what we feel.

The ability to share our feelings openly and honestly is necessary if we want to have healthy relationships with others and to be true to ourselves at the same time. When we talk about our emotions, we help others know where we're coming from on the inside, and we raise our chances of getting what we need from them.

People rely on clear communication to know how we feel about them and what we want from them. They need our help to understand us, not hints, half-truths, or silence. When we are not clear and open with others, they are left in the dark. Since we codependents have trouble communicating both our positive and our negative emotions, the people we care about often feel confused and sometimes angry when they're with us. We are not holding up our part of the relationship when we keep our feelings to ourselves so that others have to work twice as hard. Sometimes they are not willing to do that and become so frustrated that they end the relationship.

Patty and Devon have been dating for three months. Every Saturday night they go through the same conversation:

Devon: Do you feel like going to a movie or the party at Jim's house?

Patty: (Smiling) I don't know. [She really does. She would like to stay home and watch TV with Devon because she has a headache, but she's afraid he wouldn't like her choice—and he wouldn't like *her*.]

Devon: Either one is fine with me, but you decide. I'm tired of always being the one to choose what we're going to do. [He's getting frustrated.]

Patty: Seriously, I don't care. Just being with you is enough for me. It doesn't matter what we do. [She can't stand Jim or his friends, so she hopes Devon doesn't choose the party.]

Devon: I give up! We'll go to the party for a while and then see the new martial arts movie.

Patty: Sure, that sounds good. [Her voice is flat and she looks sad—she *hates* martial arts movies.]

Throughout the evening Patty sighs often and says little. When Devon asks what's wrong, she finally tells him about the headache. When he asks why she didn't tell him earlier, she responds that she didn't want to burden him. That makes Devon angry. Maybe next week he won't ask her out. Maybe he'll go out with a girl who isn't such a drag.

Sometimes we keep quiet about our feelings so much that they come out all at once in an explosion that we feel we have no control over. We can be quiet, compliant people pleasers one minute and furious blamers the next. When Devon drops Patty off at her door, he tells her to make plans for herself next weekend, since he doesn't want to date her exclusively. When she hears that she blows up, calling him names and accusing him of never thinking about her needs and feelings. "I had a miserable time tonight just as I have on all our dates," she snaps. "The only person you ever think about is yourself." Until Patty can learn to make her feelings known instead of letting them simmer until they boil over, she'll get burned in all her relationships.

There are many reasons why we codependents, like Patty, have such trouble communicating with other people. A few of them are:

- Being out of touch with our true feelings.
- Not questioning the ways we learned to relate to

other people when were growing up in our dysfunctional families.

- Not knowing how to speak up or to share our feelings because we haven't been around people who could teach us that.
- Feeling afraid that people will hate or abandon us if we disagree with them on anything, even something minor.
- Thinking we'll be a burden on others.
- Hiding our feelings of shame and unworthiness by trying to be invisible.
- Basing our self-worth on how others might react to what we have to say. (If they say no to us, we must be no good.)
- Manipulating others to do what we want them to do without taking the risk of being open about it.

COMMUNICATION GAMES CODEPENDENTS PLAY

To protect ourselves from the possibility of being hurt or shamed or abandoned by others, we devise all kinds of communication games. These games allow us to avoid being direct about our feelings and to avoid taking responsibility for them. They also often enable us to blame other people when our feelings are ignored or hurt, rather than holding ourselves accountable for refusing to speak up and share those emotions in the first place.

"If you really cared about me, you'd know how I feel!"

Because codependents spend so much time trying to figure out what other people are feeling, we expect that other people will do the same for us. Most people, unless they are codependents, too, do not play this communication game. They want us to be straightforward and to reveal our emotions rather than hiding what we feel so that they are forced to read our minds.

When people refuse to play this guessing game or when they try to read our minds and come up with the wrong answers, we feel angry. If they don't know what's bothering us, we think, we're not about to tell them. When this stage of the game fails to get us what we want, we feel hurt and even betrayed. We are convinced that if people really loved us or cared about us they would know how we felt without our having to take the risk of telling them.

Unless our friends are psychics or are extremely talented guessers, we harbor such feelings of disappointment nearly all the time. Like Patty, we expect the impossible from people and are crushed when they can't deliver it. Nobody understands us, we lament. Of course, they don't understand us; we don't give them any help!

"That will show you!"

If we are afraid of speaking our hearts and minds, and the people we know aren't into guessing games, we find ways to show how we feel without using words. We give people clues to our emotions through our actions. Patty's sighs were a clear signal to Devon that something was very wrong despite her denial of being unhappy.

More often than not, the words we use are calculated to please, but our actions convey the opposite meaning. We may say we would be happy to help a sister with the dishes when it's her turn and she needs to go out. We may even smile, but all the while we are slamming the cupboard doors nearly off their hinges. We may tell our folks that we want to try out for tennis because it will make them happy.

Then in the first game of the season we pull a muscle and can't play. We tell friends who smoke that it won't bother us if they light up in the car, then have a coughing fit.

When people pick up on our mixed messages, they don't know what to think and they get upset with us. Usually when we are confronted with those mixed messages, we deny them by telling people they didn't see what they claim to have seen. If our sister says something about the banging cupboard doors, we can safely reply, "Well, I don't know what you're complaining about. I told you I *wanted* to help you. I am *not* slamming the doors. It's your imagination." Eventually the other person gets so frustrated that she starts to argue with us. Then it's time for us to play our final card—guilt. "How could you accuse me of not wanting to help you?" we mutter. "I'm helping you, aren't I? You don't appreciate anything I do for you."

"I'm sorry, but you're stepping on my foot."

Even though it is impossible to agree with everybody all the time, many codependents give it their best shot. We tell people we're sorry even though we have done nothing to cause them hurt, discomfort, or inconvenience. In fact, we say we're sorry when other people deliberately hurt *our* feelings. It must be our fault that they are acting so nasty to us.

We may be so eager to be agreeable that we put ourselves down before other people have a chance to do so. We apologize for doing well on tests, for our new clothes, our hair, our car. If it can be named, we can find a reason to be sorry for it. It's no wonder we frequently find ourselves the target of verbal abuse. We don't go seeking the bullies of the world, but they find us anyway, as if they sense that we are the perfect targets for their verbal violence.

Often we say we are sorry when we don't really mean it simply because we think it will make people like us better. Since we are afraid of being a burden to others, we try never to ask for anything—not even their attention. We can be in a group for hours and not contribute to the conversation because we don't want to interrupt.

When we do talk, we try to think of things to say that will make those around us happy. It doesn't matter to us if our people-pleasing comments are untrue. If a friend has a piece of spinach stuck between his front teeth when he is about to give a speech, we either say nothing or we say he looks wonderful. We feel safer if he is embarrassed in front of the whole class rather than just in front of us.

"Have you heard the one about. . . ?"

When some codependents cannot squirm out of talking about their feelings any other way, they try to change the subject. In the middle of an argument or a serious discussion, if someone suddenly tells a joke (which probably isn't very funny), chances are that he or she is a codependent trying to divert attention from serious talk about feelings. The weather, the new spring fashions, automobile gas mileage—all are diversions for a codependent trying to avoid sharing feelings, even positive ones.

As soon as Linda's boyfriend asked how she felt about going steady, she started talking about how well the high school track team was doing. She was in love with him and wanted to wear his letter jacket more than anything, but telling him so embarrassed her. He asked her again, and she dropped her french fries in her lap to cause a distraction and avoid telling him her true feelings. He was convinced that she didn't want to date only him, so he didn't ask her again.

"I'm Telling On You."

Sometimes codependents find it necessary to let other people know their feelings and wishes a little more openly. Even so, rather than sitting down for a heart-to-heart talk with the person in question, we find sneakier ways that involve other people to get our points across. We may draw other people into our communication games by making them serve as go-betweens. When we're unhappy with the way a friend or family member is acting, we find another person to use as an ally, someone who will take our side. We may gossip and spread rumors or enlist someone else to tell off the person to whom we are afraid to show our anger or displeasure.

> Al was really upset with Joe for borrowing money from him and then not paying it back. Still he lent Joe money every time he asked and said nothing about how much he was owed. When he got angry enough, instead of confronting Joe with his feelings, Al complained to his other friends that Al was a moocher and used people. Eventually word got back to Joe, who then paid his debt. Because he also was a codependent, however, he did not confront Al about the backstabbing but began telling everybody how two-faced Joe was.

"Everybody's saying. . ."

Third parties need not play an active role in this game for us to use them to speak our feelings for us. We sometimes put words into their mouths. When Daniella was angry at her friend, Cynthia, for not spending much time with her since she started going out with boys, she called Cynthia on the phone. "Everybody's talking about how you're getting so stuck up," she said. "Susan and Eve and even Sherrie say you're acting like a snob. I just thought I'd tell you so you'd know how you're making them feel."

I'm telling you this for your own good."

No matter how much other people's behavior bothers codependents, they don't come right out and tell their friends or family how they're feeling. Instead they try to get people to change by acting like know-it-all experts. Doris hated to be seen with her sister because Fran was so fat. She tried avoiding her sister so she wouldn't have to say anything, but that didn't work. So Doris started checking diet books out of the library and renting exercise videos. "Being overweight is bad for your health," she told Fran. "I'm afraid you'll have a heart attack and die or something."

When we codependents tell people what they ought to do and how they should act for their own good, we slide out from taking responsibility for our true feelings. Doris avoided the issue of the shame she felt at being seen with her sister by becoming a health crusader. Most of the time such tactics fool no one. When codependents try to speak with the all-knowing voice of authority for other people's good, too often we come across as bossy and heartless manipulators, out to run people's lives and save the world.

Some codependents like to quote paragraphs out of magazine articles or, like Doris, leave books around for their erring friends to read. Or they may quote authorities on TV talk shows and toss around statistics. We hide our feelings behind reason and logic until we begin to sound like robots or computers.

When codependents are playing this game, they start their sentences with, "They say. . ." and "Everybody knows that. . ." Such intellectual bullying acts may get attention in the short run, but in the long run they fail because we come across as phonys. We are not trying to get people to change for their own good, but for *our* own good!

"It's all your fault!"

When others fail to decode our message even though we have not stated it clearly, we feel hurt and angry. Instead of owning our feelings, we either project them onto others or play a blame game, claiming that other people are *making* us feel what we feel. When we accuse other people of emotional arm twisting, we may be expressing our feelings, but we are not expressing them honestly. In effect, we are saying, "I have this feeling, but it isn't really mine. You gave it to me; now you take it back."

Usually we have stuffed our feelings for quite a while before we are moved to play the blame game. By the time we get geared up to use it, we are overly emotional and have little ability to control what we are saying. Sometimes we get so upset that we become verbally abusive, calling our friends names and accusing them of all sorts of things they didn't do. Instead of getting other people to listen to us, the blame game stops understanding and communication in their tracks. The very people we want to listen to us are so busy defending themselves against our finger-pointing that they cannot hear what we want to say to them.

"I can't hear a word you're saying!"

As codependents we often suffer from a "disease" called selective deafness. Although we encourage other people to share their thoughts and feelings with us, we have a hard time listening to everything they tell us. Instead we pay attention only to the parts we want to hear—especially when we sense that people are not responding the way we would like. Since we tend to interpret the most innocent remarks of others as an attack on our already shaky self-esteem, we shut down and do not listen.

We do not really hear what is said to us in arguments, so we respond to what we imagine people are saying or meaning. Rather than asking people what they are trying to say to us or what they are feeling, we mind read and project. It's no wonder that few of our arguments result in any real resolution or problem-solving. Instead of clearing the air, codependent arguments cloud the issue.

Unlike tennis or football or charades, codependent communication games are no fun to play. Other people get angry at us when we use them and rightly so, because we are the only ones who know the rules. If we've been codependent for very long we change those rules without warning from moment to moment. In codependent communication games, there are no winners. The people around us get frustrated, and we fail to get the understanding we want or to get our needs met.

LEARNING TO SHARE OUR FEELINGS

The only way we can win is to learn to communicate our feelings, our needs, and our wants in ways that are clear, fair, and effective. It is true that we have little control over what people will think or how they will react when we speak out, but we have even less control when we are silent about how we feel. Even though we have no guarantee that we will get our way or even be heard, we owe it to ourselves and to others to speak out.

People may disagree with us, and that is scary for codependents because our whole lives are structured to avoid conflict. Disagreements are not always a bad thing. They are not the end of the world, and they need not be the end of a relationship. When people are not in agreement but can talk and listen, they can work out compromises, solutions that make everybody a winner.

When we speak our feelings, we can own up to them rather than projecting them and blaming other people for them. Blaming and name-calling may hurt the other person's feelings and give us a temporary victory, but they do not encourage being heard. To get an idea how this works, compare the following codependent and healthy statements.

CODEPENDENT: The gossip you spread about me is ruining my life. You make me feel like dropping out of school. I can't even sleep. It's all your fault.

HEALTHY: When you gossip about me behind my back, I feel hurt.

We can also get people to listen to us by sharing our positive feelings as well as our criticisms.

CODEPENDENT: You're a jerk, and I want you to stop spreading rumors about me!

HEALTHY: You mean a lot to me, and that's
                    why I feel really hurt when you
                    spread rumors about me.

We can encourage people to listen to our feelings by
avoiding exaggerations such as *always* and *never*.

CODEPENDENT: You never tell the truth.
HEALTHY: When you said last Tuesday that
                    I was a shoplifter, that wasn't
                    truthful.

We can learn to listen to what people are saying to us
and ask for their help in understanding what they are
trying to tell us.

CODEPENDENT: Start   talking   sense.   You're
                    sounding stupid!
HEALTHY: Knowing what you mean is im-
                    portant to me and I'm not sure I
                    understand you. Could you say it
                    again?

Finally, we can be better listeners by asking people to
rephrase their thoughts in different words. And we can
reflect their thoughts back to them to be sure we have
heard them correctly.

CODEPENDENT: You don't make sense!
HEALTHY: It's important to me to under-
                    stand what you're saying. You're
                    angry at me because I promised
                    to call you last night and then
                    didn't? Is that right?

Expressing our feelings keeps us from becoming emotionally paralyzed to the point of being unable to relate— even to ourselves. That's why it is important to admit our mistakes soon after we have made them. If we don't express our regret, our guilt turns into shame. And when we're upset with people or our feelings are hurt, we need to talk about it *before* our anger or hurt hardens into resentment that may lead to a big blow-up later.

It is also important to know that we need not express ourselves immediately in every situation. We may need to take some time to figure out exactly how we feel before we make a snap decision about what we're going to do about those emotions. Before we can talk straight, we have to be able to think and feel straight, so we may need to ask for time out in the discussion to collect our thoughts and feelings.

Since discussions of feelings work best when both people are relatively rested and not pressured, sometimes we need to plan them. When your friend has to catch a plane and the last boarding call has been announced, that is not the time to talk about how you're smothered by the relationship. When you have failed your English grammar test, the middle of the teacher's lecture is not the time to bring up your hurt, shock, and humiliation. When your mother is drunk, a heart-to-heart discussion of how you feel about her alcoholism will not be productive. A good way to handle these situations is to let the person know you want to talk later, set a time, and try your best to stick to it.

Sometimes you may choose not to share your feelings, and that's healthy, too, because it is a conscious decision on your part. Every human being needs privacy, and that includes private thoughts and feelings. Even though expressing your emotions is a healthy way of relating, it doesn't mean you have to express every thought or feeling.

As you start dealing with your feelings and practicing expressing them, you'll soon get a sense of what is important to share and what thoughts and feelings you want to keep to yourself.

We need to keep in mind, as well, that other people will not necessarily want to listen to us. Sometimes they can't or won't offer us understanding, and that is their right. When such lack of understanding happens, it may have nothing to do with us. Perhaps the person has had a bad day or is struggling with problems. The fact that someone doesn't care how we feel doesn't mean that we don't or shouldn't feel that emotion. When we express ourselves and are usually ignored or made fun of, we need to take care of ourselves by finding people who *will* listen to us and who *can* show empathy.

Expressing feelings openly and honestly is not always easy even for people who are not codependent. Be kind to yourself by speaking up one step at a time. You might begin slowly by expressing an opinion in a class discussion. Or you could tell someone that you like what she is wearing today. Sometimes we need to practice on small feeling issues before we can work up to the big feeling issues that we need to talk about eventually. That's fine.

You are already writing about your emotions in your journal. Now is a good time to start writing about speaking out. You can jot down whether or not you chose to express yourself, how you did it, and what happened. Every time you express yourself, write about how you felt beforehand and afterward. What did you say? How did the other person respond? By writing, you can be more in touch with your feelings about sharing feelings. You can also shape what you want to say and practice saying it.

Another tactic you can try is to role-play communication scenes with a friend. Act out past situations that made you feel anger or betrayal or jealousy, or make up new ones. Since codependents have a tough time expressing affection, you might want to choose some positive emotions to work with, too. Imagine the feeling, then practice talking about it to your friend and listening to what he or she has to say in return. Record your conversation on a tape, and listen to see what you did that was effective and what you may need to improve. With some practice and a little coaching, you'll be well on your way to speaking out and being a communication winner.

CHAPTER 8

Learning to Trust

Trust is the basis of strong, positive relationships, but codependents learn early in life not to trust. That defense helped us to survive emotionally in our families, so we are afraid to drop it even when it keeps us isolated.

When Brady was a little kid his father, an alcoholic, would promise to take him to ball games but then get drunk and pass out an hour or two before the game began. He vowed to Brady he would be there for him whenever his son needed him, but as it turned out he was drinking with his friends when Brady played Little League games, when he needed advice, and much later when he got his driver's license.

No matter how sincere those promises were, Brady knew he couldn't count on his father. Even though Brady didn't stop loving him, he stopped trusting him. It was the only way he could protect himself against disappointment and feelings of betrayal. Today he has plenty of friends, but none of them are really close, and every year or so he seems to dump the old ones and get new ones. It's safer, he thinks, not to depend on people too much—they're just going to hurt you.

Not only do codependents learn early that other people are untrustworthy, we learn to distrust ourselves, too.

Carol was twelve when she began suspecting that her mother was having an affair with a man at work. She stayed later and later at the office and came home with wine on her breath, but Carol and her father both pretended everything was as usual. Once when Carol was looking in her mother's purse for bus fare she found books of matches from several hotels.

Then came the day when she and her friends ditched school to go shopping downtown, and she saw her mother smiling and holding hands with a stranger in a restaurant. That night when Carol confronted her, her mother said she was seeing things. Maybe she was crazy and should make an appointment with a psychiatrist. If Carol really loved her, how could she make up such lies? To this day, Carol does not trust herself to believe what she sees, hears, or feels. She is afraid to make friends or to go out with boys. She worries that if she does get close to another person, her imagination might run wild as it did with her mother or that her friends might lie to her. It's safer to stay at home and watch videos.

Brady and Carol both learned to put up high walls between themselves and other people to defend against possible hurt. For both of them, as for most codependents, the wall went up one brick at a time. Every time a codependent experiences pain in a relationship, we add another brick to the wall. Since we often don't know our own feelings, or don't speak them, we get into situations with people that leave us emotionally bruised and battered. By the time we are teenagers the wall may be so high that neither we nor others can climb it to form an emotionally intimate relationship. The defenses that worked for us when we were younger begin to hurt us.

Like Brady, we may become compulsive collectors of people without ever knowing them very well or revealing our thoughts to them. Or like Carol, we may escape from relating to other people into a world of television or books or even drugs. Whether we surround ourselves with people or run from relating, we often cannot admit that our walls exist. Instead we tell ourself that it's better to have lots of acquaintances than a few close friends, or that it's better to date somebody different every week than to get serious about one person for a while. We may judge our relationships in terms of quantity rather than quality, determining our self-worth by our popularity at any given moment. Because we give others so much power over how we feel about ourselves, we need them. At the same time we can't afford to get too close lest they find out what we're really like and drop us.

Even if we spend most of our time alone, we still fall into the codependent trap of living through other people and letting them determine how we feel about ourselves. In this case, we have decided ahead of time that people will not like us, so we refuse to interact with them and give them the chance to reject us. Eventually we may feel lonely and unloved a great deal of the time. We are so used to living with our walls that we forget that the walls are what keep others away from us. Before we know it we start feeling shame about our difficulties with people. Something must be horribly wrong with us not to have close and lasting friendships.

NO TRESPASSING—KEEP OUT

If we could get past our walls or tear them down, the chances are good that we would have friends. More often than not, though, the barriers we put up to guard against feeling pain are posted all over with big no-trespassing signs—signs that everyone reads and heeds. Soon what started out as a protective blockade to keep people partly or completely out becomes a barrier to our growth. We may deny that our walls exist, but they have turned into a prison, caging our true self or inner child. By mistrusting others without ever giving them a chance to prove they are worthy of our trust, we cut ourselves off from the flow of life.

No matter how much we deny the basic fact of our loneliness and delude ourselves that we are perfectly fine being isolated from the rest of the world, our inner child knows the truth. We may tell ourselves that we're shy, and that we were born that way—there's nothing we can do about it. When others approach us, we make them carry the entire burden of conversation, or we arm ourselves with insulting and critical remarks as sharp as a porcupine's quills. We may tell ourselves that we are nonconformists and would hate it if we did fit in, and then we purposely act in off-putting ways to scare people away. Or we feel morally superior to other people: We're good, and they're bad. We're right, and they're wrong. We're mature, and they're just babies.

We may convince ourselves that we're smarter than our families and classmates. Certainly we would not want to lower ourselves to be friends with a bunch of dummies. Carl ran that kind of a con job on himself. Even though he knew it irritated his classmates and his teachers, he monopolized class discussions. When other students could squeeze in a word, he put them down and corrected them. He lay in wait for his teachers to make a mistake so that he could show off his intelligence. No wonder nobody would have anything to do with Carl. Who wants to be friends with a person whose sole pleasure in life is to correct other people's pronunciation and grammar? Carl was convinced, however, that people were jealous of his knowledge. Despite the fact that classmates with higher grades and test scores had plenty of friends, Carl was content with his self-delusion. It kept him from having to do anything about the wall.

When codependents like Carl do bump into the wall, they are sometimes shocked by the bruising loneliness they feel. No matter how hard we try to convince ourselves that we don't need or want anybody else in our world, the truth is that human beings function best when their lives are a balance between being alone and being emotionally connected with other people. Life in loneliness not only is boring but can be emotionally scarring. Even when we are with groups of people, we feel excluded, as though we just don't fit in. We can feel like strangers within our own families or even in romantic relationships. Yet though we may want to reach out to form friendships, we are not quite certain how to do it.

Sometimes when we try to be close to others and fail to connect, we're stunned, as if we had banged our heads against a wall. It hurts deeply to have people not notice us or reject us completely. It's painful to feel that we don't have a friend in the world, no one to share our joys and our sorrows, no one to help us when we need it, no one to joke around with or test our our ideas on. All human beings need to feel loved and as if they belong. When codependents try and fail at friendship, that gives us an excuse to build the wall even higher.

Our trouble making and keeping close friends is compounded by the fact that we may have grown up in families that were isolated. Many dysfunctional families cut themselves off from all but trivial contact with outsiders. They may smile and nod at the mailman or have business acquaintances, but emotionally intimate friendships are usually forbidden. If people got too close, they might find out the family secrets. Since we haven't seen our parents form friendships with people outside our immediate families, we may not have a clue how to form friendships of our own. We never saw people offering invitations, making small talk, and certainly not sharing feelings. We may have heard warnings from our parents about not forming close emotional ties with outsiders:

- Other people will take advantage of you.
- People are just out to use you.
- Don't accept kindness form others; you'll be obligated to them.
- Be completely independent.

Perhaps, too, we were discouraged from having much contact with other kids. If one or both of our parents had a problem with drugs or alcohol or was emotionally unstable, we might have felt ashamed to bring kids home. We never knew what would be going on, and we didn't want outsiders to see what our families were really like. Now that we want to make friends, we have very little practice at it, so we feel awkward or clumsy. Those uncomfortable feelings of not knowing quite what to do add yet another layer of bricks to the wall.

GO AWAY CLOSER

Whether we codependents are just starting to make friends or already know many people but are not close to them, our lack of trust can make those relationships very difficult to maintain. We are never quite sure how much of ourselves we want to share with other people and how much we should allow them to give to us. When people are nice to us, our first thoughts are often, "What do they want from me? Is this a trick?" We may begin a relationship with a happy, trusting heart, then suddenly end it abruptly because the more we care, the more we think we will be hurt. Our lack of trust combined with our habit of not talking about our feelings can puzzle other people, pushing them away and deepening our feeling of isolation.

Ramona had liked Steve for months and spent a great deal of time dreaming about what it would be like to go out with him. It was clear that he was attracted to her, too. But when he began smiling at her, talking to her in the halls, and eating lunch at the table where she always sat in the cafeteria, she got scared. So sometimes she froze him out and hurried away, and at other times, when her positive feelings won, she smiled back and even flirted. Finally he asked her out to the moives, and she was thrilled to accept. Then her fear kicked in, and she told him she couldn't go; something had come up. He asked her out once more, and she did the same thing. Obviously hurt, he never approached her again. How could he know that it was Ramona's fear and basic lack of trust in people that made her act in confusing and hurtful ways? He thought she was deliberately playing games and making fun of him.

Another way codependents keep friends at a distance is to be generous—generous to a fault! We give of our time and our energy and our talents. We lend people money, help them with their homework, and listen to their problems. But when they try to give us things and do favors for us, we cut them off.

On the outside it may seem that we are being givers out of the goodness of our hearts; inside we are adding up what others owe us. We expect them to pay that secret debt, but we never allow them to because we don't trust enough to be open and accepting of what they offer. We harbor grudges against people because they are not giving us what we refuse to take. We're sure they are using us. And we use those grudges as yet another reason not to trust. Putting people in positions where they seem selfish, where they are obligated to us, is an effective insurance policy against the give and take of emotional intimacy.

We may distance ourselves from people by including so many others in our lives and becoming so busy that we never have time to sit down for a meaningful talk with anyone. We use others to boost our self-esteem, and when we have used them up we dump them and go on to new friendships. We may pick a fight as an excuse to end a relationship or start focusing on flaws so that we can no longer stand to be around the person. Even though people-collecting codependents may be envied for the number of folks they hang out with, they still trust no one. Their popularity is mostly an act; inside they are as lonely as the codependents who act like loners. Their telephones ring constantly, their calendars are filled with fun things to do, but their lives are empty of meaningful contact with other people.

WHOM DO YOU TRUST?

As long as we do not trust ourselves, we cannot trust other people. Because we codependents depend on other people to meet our need for self-esteem, we are afraid they will betray our trust and hurt us. Without the approval of others, we believe we might not exist. We want other people to take care of us, to meet our needs and to make our shame go away, but we believe we must be completely independent and do everything for ourselves. It is no wonder that we bounce back and forth between completely rejecting other people and clinging to them so tightly we emotionally smother them.

We ache inside to trust, and we are terrified of trusting. We have no idea whom we can trust and under what circumstances. Often our suspicions about the motives of those around us arise because we mistrust our own judgment about other people. Many times we act out those internal conflicts with other people by giving them mixed messages—we tell them to go away closer.

Sometimes we stay isolated for long periods of time, then find ourselves attracted to people who really are untrustworthy. When we crawl out from behind the wall to have a relationship with a cruel or inappropriate person, we eventually get hurt, especially since we give significant others the power to confirm or deny us as worthwhile human beings.

Hugh was a high school senior and he was so painfully shy that he still had not asked a girl out on a date. He knew Sharon was a flirt and that she dated guys and dumped them, but he had had a secret crush on her for two years. He believed that if he could just get her to go to the prom with him, his life would change. Mustering all his courage, he asked her, and she laughed in his face. Soon he was the school joke. Hugh resolved he would never ask another girl out as long as he lived.

When we have bad experiences like Hugh's, we tell ourselves we knew it would happen. You can't trust anybody. We never stop to think that we may be setting ourselves up for failure by trying to connect with people who really don't want anything to do with us, while we ignore those who do. Focusing on cold or emotionally distant people allows us to keep our wall intact without taking responsibility for building it. Our hurt feelings are all the other person's fault, we tell ourselves. After we are rejected, we isolate ourselves once more until we get so desperate to connect that we grab the first person who comes along, and the vicious circle starts all over again.

To overcome our lack of trust, we need to find the middle path between dependency, or people addiction, and isolated independence. That road is called *inter-dependence*. It involves learning to figure out who is worthy of our trust and who is not, as well as being able to gauge how far we can trust others. Interdependence also requires that we learn to balance our relationships so we can be both givers and takers. It requires that we do not look to others to build up our shaky self-esteem, but do recognize that people are an important part of our lives.

Because codependents have an all-or-nothing attitude about trust, we need to learn that relationships have a gradual and natural pattern of unfolding and that healthy relationships need to be worked at—they don't happen magically. Long-lasting friendships and dating relationships start with people trusting each other a little bit. Based on the words and actions that follow, that trust gradually begins to build.

Too often we codependents want fantasy friendships where intimacy and total trust come instantly. If that does not happen, we may write off potential friends as being cold and distant when they really are not that way. Because of our all-or-nothing thinking, we may feel we have to trust people totally or not at all. In truth, there are many degrees of trust. Some people we might trust with our money, our lives, and our deepest secrets. Others we trust less. Some people are not worthy of our trust at all. We can trust people without loving them, and we can love people, especially our dysfunctional family members, without trusting them.

LEARNING TO TRUST

Self-trust is critical to taking care of ourselves in relationships with others. If we take time to pay attention to our perceptions of people, we know on our inner-child or true-self level whether or not we should trust them. When we trust ourselves and act toward others based on that inner knowing, most of the time we can avoid situations where betrayal and violation of our trust are a given. Even when we are hurt by others, we can recover from our emotional wounds more easily. We know that the friendships we attempt are not the last we will have.

Although we can practice self-trust alone, we cannot learn to trust others when we isolate ourselves in our room or behind our invisible wall. We must have other people with whom to practice connecting skills.

Support groups or rap groups are one good way of learning to trust others in a safe environment. Talking with a high school counselor or a peer counselor can be another. Theses options are useful to recovery because groups and counseling situations have rules to help foster trust. People are there to help one another, not to criticize. Group members and counselors promise not to carry gossip outside of the room. It is understood that these relationships are conducted with healthy rules and no dysfunctional family games are allowed. Some support groups for codependents are listed at the end of this book. You can find out about support, rap, or peer counseling groups in your area by contacting these national organization or by checking with a school counselor.

Eventually groups are not enough, and we feel a need to form closer friendships with some of the people we see during the course of our daily lives. Even though we may feel scared and exposed when we take the risk of tearing down that top layer of the barrier that keeps us from emotionally intimate relationships, it can be done. Making friends comes easiest when we place ourselves in situations with people who share some of our interests. There are lots of things you can do to help the process along:

- Smile and say, "Hi," to someone you sit next to in class, rather than waiting for the person to speak to you first.
- Give someone an honest compliment.
- Ask a question that requires more than a yes or no answer.
- Get involved in sports.
- Join an after-school committee or club.
- Attend a youth group at your church or temple.
- Volunteer.
- Sign up for a class at a recreation center or an adult-education class at a community college.

- Find a part-time job where you'll be working with kids your own age.

We can keep track of our progress in learning to trust ourselves and others by writing our thoughts, feelings, and experiences about friendships in our journals. It might be interesting to make a list of every person you know and rank them in order of how well you know them. Have you been too distrustful of others and put them off? Or have you been trusting everybody and being victimized and hurt? Are there people you would like to know better but have been afraid to approach? Try some of the friendship-starting tactics listed above and write what happens in your journal.

As we work on learning to trust, codependents need to remember that not everyone will want to be our friend. That's okay. Plenty of people will, once they get to know us. We need to remember, too, that for us opening up to share ourselves and trusting in any way are big risks. We need to take them slowly. Just as we would not expect to be able to climb Mt. Everest without training for it, we can't expect to climb our wall and feel confident making friends unless we work up to the task.

Finally, we need to be optimistic, something many codependents find hard to do. It is time to trade our doom and gloom scenarios for brighter, more trusting pictures of our ability to connect with others. As our self-confidence grows stronger, our wall will start to crumble and we will be free from our self-imposed isolation. There's a whole world out there waiting for us to explore it.

CHAPTER ◇ 9

Setting Boundaries

C odependents do not hide behind their wall all the time. We have to come out to have relationships once in a while because we rely on other people to provide us with feelings of self-worth. We tend either to isolate or to form intense bonds with others. Rarely are these friendships based on give and take or mutual sharing. We have an incredibly difficult time starting and keeping relationships in which the balance of power is equal. In some relationships we give all the power to the other person, and in others we try to keep all the power for ourselves. Sometimes we do both in one relationship and play tug-of-war.

Our partnership problems can be so big that some recovering codependents joke that in the past they didn't have relationships; they took hostages or were taken hostage. This tendency to fuse with others so that we lose our individuality and demand that others do the same causes major friction between us and the people we befriend. All that conflict and tension can turn our own lives into a battleground, too.

Relationships, for us, are made up of extreme highs and

lows with little middle ground. When codependents are not pushing other people away with a vengeance, we are clinging to them in desperation, needy and greedy for their attention. Because we rely completely on other people for a sense of wholeness, we hang on to them for dear life—often with a choke-hold. Many times we ignore the emotional boundaries that separate us. We start confusing the other person's wants and needs with our own. If the relationship ever ended, we believe, we couldn't survive. Eventually we come to view the people we are relating to as extensions of ourselves, much like our arms or legs, and the threat of losing control over them or losing them entirely is very frightening.

Penny and Michelle have been best friends ever since elementary school. Now in tenth grade, they still try to take all of their classes together and call each other at least once a day after school. When they go out with boys, they always double-date. The kids at school tease them and call them the twins, but the joke is getting stale, at least for Michelle. She likes sports and wants to try out for the track team, but Penny, who hates sports, has persuaded her to give up the idea. She considers Michelle's new interest a sign of betrayal. Instead of providing the support it did for both of them in the past, the girls' friendship is like a straitjacket keeping Michelle from growing.

Randy never thought about using drugs—after all, dope was for dopes. Then his next-door neighbor, Dave, who was two grades ahead, began smoking marijuana. Randy had looked up to Dave over the years; the older boy had taken him for rides in his car and once even let him drive before he was old enough to get a license. When Dave offered him the first joint, Randy had a coughing fit and didn't like the way it made him feel. Despite the fact that grass gave him splitting headaches, he started using it regularly. If he refused, he thought, Dave wouldn't have anything to do with him. Even though the two teenagers were not really friends, Randy couldn't stand the thought of Dave's thinking he was a wimp; that might mean he really was one. By giving Dave the power to add to or take away from his self-worth, Randy put himself in the position of going against his own values.

Carla gets exhausted when she hangs out with Roger; he is one of the most negative and irresponsible people she can imagine existing. But for super-responsible Carla a boy like that is a challenge. Roger always forgets to do his homework, he doesn't return phone calls, and he has so many unpaid traffic tickets that the police came after him. Still Carla makes a point of calling him several times a week and eating lunch with him, even though he has clearly stated he wants nothing from her but sex. So far she has held out, but she feels sorry for this "bad boy" and has turned him into her project. If she is understanding and patient enough, he'll give in and accept her kindness. Once that happens, she is sure she can turn his life around. Carla does not realize that her obsession with reforming Roger, who doesn't really like her, keeps her away from healthy relationships with guys who *would* like her and treat her with love and respect.

Whether we keep those we care about from being who they are, do things that go against our own beliefs to make someone like us, or attach ourselves to emotionally wounded people who will only use us, codependents are people who *need* people. If someone likes us, anyone likes us, we must be okay—at least sort of okay.

No matter how compulsively we collect people, they never quite manage to give us the self-worth and self-acceptance we expect. And thus many of our relationships are doomed to disappointment. Nobody else can give us self-esteem. Even though we may feel great pain and frustration because of this, instead of giving up and looking inside we work twice as hard at being the best possible friend or relative in the world. No matter how frantically or how long we fight to be the perfect companion, we can't reach that goal because we have not yet learned to be our *own* best friend. In fact, we are in a tug-of-war with ourselves, one that mirrors what is going on in our relationships.

When we codependents come out from behind our wall, we usually have no trouble attracting people. We are the ones who don't hesitate to put aside our own homework to help others with theirs or give them a ride at a moment's notice when their car breaks down. If they happen to mention that they like tomatoes, we give them every last tomato wedge on our taco salad even though we like the tomatoes best, too. We're the kind of people others turn to when they need someone to listen to their family troubles, their dating disasters, or their struggle to choose a career. When people we care about argue with each other, we may find ourselves drawn into the middle as peacemakers.

Our tact and patience, our politeness and empathy for other people are wonderful qualities to have. So are our abilities to nurture people, to help them, and to be generous. Our problem is that we carry those virtues too far, often doing for others at our own expense. Because we do not balance our caretaking qualities with a healthy dose of self-interest, we often feel that our energy is being used up or drained dry by other people.

We would not have such sticky relationship problems if what was best for others was always what was best for us, but the world doesn't work that way. When codependents have to make a choice, usually we put the needs or wants of other people ahead of everything else. Like Michelle, we give up our dreams, or, like Randy, we do things that make us feel very uncomfortable. We may choose people who are all wrong for us, as Carla did, because we are sure it's our job to take care of even those who may hurt us.

Because we put everyone else's needs and feelings before our own, we start to live *through* others rather than living our own lives. Once we form close relationships with others, we forget where we leave off and they begin. How they feel becomes far more important to us than how we feel. We project our emotions onto them and become consumed with trying to read their minds and hearts. In the meantime, we don't pay any attention to our own minds and hearts. Our inner child is just as lonely and ignored as ever.

Most of us who are codependents never learned to set boundaries that define who we are and who we are not, what behavior we will tolerate from others, and what behavior we will not tolerate. We say yes when we really want to say no. We let people take advantage of us or even dictate to us what to think and feel.

Other times we have trouble respecting the boundaries other people set. We try to boss them around or manipulate them into doing what we want them to do, and often we fail to respect their individuality and right to privacy. We're afraid that if we let people we care about be themselves they'll leave us for good.

Relationships without boundaries are called *enmeshment*. That is because our emotions and needs are so entangled with those of the other person that we are tied up in knots. After all, when we depend on someone other than ourselves to provide us with feelings of self-worth, we cannot afford to see ourselves as independent from them or to see them as independent from us—no matter how bad things get.

We know we are enmeshed when we feel trapped, when we feel a great deal of emotional pain, and we blame the other person—but we stay with the person anyway. When we stop to think about how we really feel about that person, often we are confused. Do we really like the person, or do we stay in the relationship just because we believe we need it? Do we keep the person in our life because of positive feelings, or do we remain loyal to avoid being alone?

People who are enmeshed with each other have a tough time knowing how they feel, and they have an even tougher time communicating with each other and solving their problems. Instead of really talking with our friends, we hold imaginary conversations with them. We try to second-guess them, to anticipate what they want from us, and we are sure we know them better than they know themselves. When friends who are enmeshed disagree, they go around in circles, repeating the same old negative patterns over and over again.

To untangle our enmeshed relationships with other people, we need to set clearly defined boundaries. Our boundaries must be flexible so that we can open up and let people get close to us or keep them at a distance. Flexible boundaries give us room to grow. They enable us to make appropriate choices based on people and situations, instead of being locked into one way of relating to everybody we meet.

It helps if we can see healthy boundaries as something like the fence around a yard. We need to make our boundaries sturdy enough to avoid being completely defenseless or vulnerable and tough enough to keep passersby from trespassing on our private property and trampling the flowerbeds. At the same time we don't want the fence to be like a prison wall, so high we can't see over it or have a conversation over it. It helps, too, to build gates so that we can invite people in and let them leave when we want more privacy.

We codependents sometimes have boundaries that look like healthy boundaries—right down to the gates. The only problem is that our gates open and close only from the outside. When we want to be with friends or we want to be left alone, there is little we can do about it if we can't open or close the gate. Without a latch or a knob on the inside, our boundaries are still being defined by those around us. We have no defense against being emotionally invaded and hurt. Neither can we open up to emotionally intimate relationships when we choose to do so.

Another way of thinking about boundaries is to picture

NO RELATIONSHIP	CODEPENDENT RELATIONSHIP	HEALTHY RELATIONSHIP

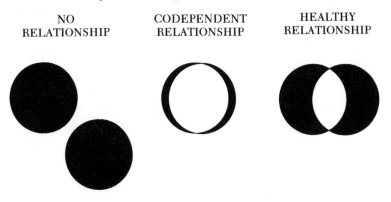

them as circles. When we are trapped behind walls or when we choose not to have a relationship with another person, the perimeters of our boundaries do not touch. In enmeshed, codependent relationships, our circle almost covers the other person's. Neither of us has much privacy or breathing room. In a healthy relationship our boundary circles overlap. We are able to share and interact while remaining our own person.

THE DOORMAT DILEMMA

Contrary to the song, people who need people are not the luckiest people in the world—we are often dependent victims both of circumstances and of other people. That is because we *do not* set limits and we *do* crave approval and affection from others to fill the empty space where our self-esteem should be. In effect we become doormats, allowing and sometimes even inviting others to walk all over us.

Margaret had been going out with Darren for three months before he hit her the first time. Sure, he had always insisted on having his way, and when he was angry he had called her names. But he had never been violent until the night they went to a party and he accused her of flirting with her cousin's old boyfriend. She had only been *talking* to the boy, and she said so. Darren, who had had more than a few too many beers, continued to argue later in the car. That's when he punched her in the arm and slapped her face.

   Instead of breaking off with him, Margaret kept dating Darren because she knew he needed help. Probably he had hit her, she thought, because he was mad at his alcoholic mother. Besides, she really loved him; he made her feel special and taken care of, emotions she hadn't felt since her parents had divorced and she had gone to live with her grandparents. Still, no matter how loving and understanding Margaret tried to be, Darren's anger and abuse grew stronger. It wasn't until he broke he arm when she was late picking him up from work that she stopped seeing him; and that was only because her grandparents forbade it after the hospital social worker stepped in. Even then, she was more concerned about the breakup than her broken arm.

Our emotional neediness and lack of boundaries serve as an open invitation to invasion, especially by the bullies of the world. In Margaret's case, the fact that she depended on Darren to feel cared for meant that she tolerated his abusive behavior. Instead of making a decision based on what would be good for her, she focused all her attention on trying to understand him. Certainly she had not asked for beatings, and she didn't deserve them. No one deserves to be treated that way—ever! What Margaret *did not* do was to set limits on what behavior she would tolerate from a boyfriend. Without pulling back into herself, looking inside and creating healthy boundaries to protect herself, she never thought about leaving Darren and never really questioned his abusive behavior.

Invasions by other people are not always as dramatic as hitting or slapping. Threats of physical violence can be assault, too. If someone threatens to break your neck if you don't shut up, that's emotional abuse. People can victimize us by destroying our property, by calling us names, or by making untrue negative remarks about us. Stepping in and trying to control our lives is another way bullies have of victimizing us. One of our friends may try to tell us what people we can and cannot have as friends. They may dictate to us what classes to take, or how to dress, or what music to listen to.

LIVING IN YOUR OWN SKIN

The opposite side of giving control over our lives to other people is trying to control their lives. Since we don't respect our boundaries, it's impossible for us to respect those of other human beings. We codependents may not punch people out or even threaten to; we're much too nice for that. We may not call people names or say mean things, but we *are* experts at bossiness. We always know what the people around us *should* be thinking and what they *ought* to be doing. When we don't tell them outright, we find ways to manipulate them into being the way we want them to be.

Because of our insecurities, controlling others makes us feel wanted and needed. It also gives us a false sense of safety. Thinking we can take power over our lives by taking power over other people seldom works in the long run. Often it backfires. We find *ourselves* being controlled to the point of obsession by the very people whose lives we are trying to run.

We do not always start out deliberately living in other people's skins and trying to make people do things our way. More often than not, we learned to manipulate in our dysfunctional families. There controlling was a technique we saw people using much of the time. It also may have seemed the only way to survive the stress and uncertainty that confronted us nearly every day.

Kit's mother drinks only two or three times a week, but everytime she does pour herself a glass of wine to "relax," she ends up finishing the whole bottle. Then she gets very angry and often yells at her daughter for no reason. Since she was a little girl, Kit has begged her mother to get help, but that hasn't worked. If only she could get her mother to change, she thinks, her family would be a happy one. So when her mother brings home a bottle of wine Kit either tries to hide it or invents an emergency to distract her mother from drinking. Once she even sprained her ankle on purpose because she knew she would have to be driven to the doctor's office and her mother couldn't drink there. Kit's thoughts constantly center around the alcohol problem and how to end it. She is sure that there is a way to make her mother stop and that if she thinks long and hard enough she'll find it.

Among the methods we codependents use most often to get others to be the way we want them to be are the following.

People-pleasing. When we tell people what we think they want to hear no matter what we are *really* thinking and feeling, we are trying to manipulate them into liking us. We pretend to be what we are not, voicing agreement when we disagree in order to avoid conflict and to prevent people from leaving us. When we try to control people's moods and what they think about us to the extent that we feed them false information about our feelings, we are not being true to ourselves. In the end, we are hurt most deeply by people-pleasing deceptions because we are selling ourselves short.

Being instantly intimate. Sometimes codependents crave closeness so much that we overwhelm people, crashing through their boundaries like tanks smashing through fences in old war movies. We spend every minute we can with them, and when we can't be with them, we call. Ignoring their privacy boundaries, we quiz them about the details of their lives. We share our problems with them whether they want to listen or not. Demanding fierce loyalty, we can be jealous to the point of insisting that our new friends give up their other friendships, their hobbies, and their schoolwork. In romantic relationships, we may trade sex for approval and emotional closeness long before we are really ready, or we may demand that trade from others.

Caretaking.   We confuse caring about people for taking care of them. Often we try to help people when they neither want nor need it. Other times we hook up with people who really do need help, and we give so much of it that we keep them dependent on us. Even though our caretaking may seem like a generous act on the surface, we may really be using it to buy loyalty or affection that we don't think we deserve or could get any other way. In the process, we rob people of the chance to take responsibility for themselves.

Fixing.   After a while simply taking care of people and meeting their needs isn't enough. We go a step further in invading their boundaries by trying to change or to fix them. Some of us become part-time counselors, diagnosing our friends' problems and handing out advice. Others are reformers, trying to manipulate people into stopping drinking or smoking or into getting better grades. We are experts at nagging, pleading, cajoling, and whining. When people complain about our tactics, we say we are doing it for their own good. Usually the opposite is true. Since we have given control over our own lives to them, we mistakenly believe that letting us boss them around and make their decisions for them is a fair trade.

Playing guilt games. Instead of owning up to the anger we feel when our manipulations fail to work, codependents walk around hurt and sad. Often we are filled with resentment and we express it by going into a poor-pitiful-me routine rather than looking at how we might change. We wonder now our friends can treat us this way when we have done so much for them. When we were kids, we may have watched a parent play the martyr role and manipulate through guilt, or we may have found out that pouting got us our way, and so we use it today. When people won't do things for us, we invade their boundaries by saying that if they really cared about us they would do our homework or give us a ride to school.

Learning to Set Boundaries

Since many of us grew up in families that were enmeshed, we need to know that it is more than okay to set boundaries between us and other people, it's a matter of self-survival. Learning to notice and respect the boundaries other people have established is a matter of relationship survival. Once we have begun to deal with our shame and feelings of unworthiness, once we have begun nurturing ourselves emotionally, we are ready to detach ourselves from dependency on other people and to start figuring out where they leave off and we begin.

Just where *do* we begin and end? We can start to answer that question by taking a look at our comfort zones, the emotional spaces most comfortable to keep between ourselves and others in our lives. A map of our comfort zones might look something like this:

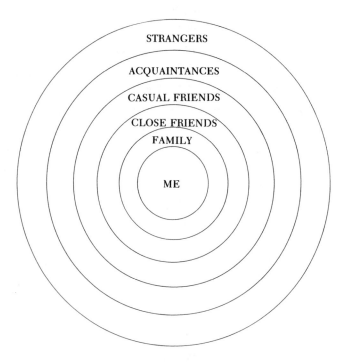

Try drawing such a map in your journal. Your map may be different, because some of us feel closer to our best friends than to our family members. That's perfectly okay.

Once you have drawn your map, you can fill it in with things you feel comfortable sharing with the people in each zone. Some of those things might be:

- The most personal secret you would share.
- The most personal secret you would feel comfortable hearing from them.
- How you would feel happiest spending your time with them.

- The most you would want to show your feelings to them.
- A personal belonging that you could let them borrow without feeling used.
- The most critical remark you could hear from them and not be extremely upset.
- The biggest favor you could do for them without feeling resentment.
- The level of physical contact with them that you would not feel was an invasion.

Once we have a clear picture of our boundaries, we need to know how to defend them assertively but in a way that does not attack or invade others. We need to learn say no to others or to let them know that they have gone too far into our comfort zone. The healthiest way to do that is with clear and direct communication instead of manipulation. Some methods of doing it are:

- Saying no in a firm but polite voice.
- Letting people know we can still like them and say no to something they want us to do.
- Keeping our explanations short and easy to understand.
- Using "I" to own up to what we want instead of blaming others for making us feel the way we do or projecting our feelings onto them.
- Asking for what we want, whether it's a hug or a favor, instead of suffering in silence.
- Respecting the rights of others to say no to our requests.
- Learning to really listen to what other people say about their feelings.
- Admitting our own mistakes when we make them.

- Paying attention to when it is and is not appropriate for us to have heart-to-heart conversations.

Clear communication is not complicated. In fact, it is a lot easier than trying to manipulate other people and feeling that they are manipulating us. Because most of us codependents are not used to asking for what we need or refusing the needs others ask us to meet, we must practice our assertiveness skills.

One way of doing that is to get a friend to help you role-play as you did when you practiced sharing your feelings. Your friend could ask you for favors such as borrowing your car or copying answers from you on a test. Then you can practice saying things like: "I don't want to lose you as a friend, but, no, you can't borrow my car. My insurance won't cover you." Be sure to reverse roles, too, so you can learn to ask for what you want and gain experience being turned down—and hearing yes!

Finally, be sure to keep track of how you're doing in your journal. Healthy boundaries grow slowly. By writing down how we feel about what is going on, we get some useful clues about our comfort zones. In the privacy of our journal we can learn to notice when we are feeling controlled and when we are trying to boss other people around. When we find either of those things happening, we may want to go back to our boundary maps and revise them.

Learning to say no to other people can feel pretty scary. So can learning to *hear* no from those we care about. Developing those two boundary-setting and boundary-respecting skills is worth the effort. They are the only way we can finally say yes to healthy relationships—and *mean* it!

CHAPTER ◇ 10

Taking Charge of
Your Life

C onnecting with your inner child, conquering shame, dealing with feelings, speaking out, learning to trust, setting boundaries—it takes a lot of work to recover from codependency. Most of the time we keep moving forward as we work through our personal recovery process, but sometimes codependents feel as if we are stuck or are taking several steps back for every one we take forward.

It is tough to avoid feeling like a failure when that happens. After all, codependents are perfectionists, and we are experts at putting ourselves down. Instead of focusing on our progress, we may decide to give up on our recovery as the old, self-shaming tapes begin to play in our mind. When that happens, it is all too easy to fall back into the patterns of blaming other people for "making" us feel and do things, for "making" us who we are today. One of the most tempting ways to do this is blaming our parents.

Parent-bashing is a trap that even adults who are recovering from codependency sometimes find hard to avoid.

When Andrew got fed up with the hard time he had keeping friends and the helplessness he felt both at school and at work, he joined a self-help group for teens with an alcoholic parent. Right away he began feeling better about himself, and for the first time in years he began to hope that his future could be brighter than his past. It wasn't long, however, before his old hopelessness overtook him and his recovery stopped. This time instead of blaming himself for all his "bad luck," he blamed his family.

"What can you expect from me?" he asked his Spanish teacher when he failed a test. "I'm the child of an alcoholic." When a girl he wanted to take out said she had other plans, Andrew told himself that if it were not for his dysfunctional family he could date any girl he wanted to ask. "If you two weren't so screwed up, I'd be okay today," he yelled at his parents after the police had stopped and ticketed him for speeding. Since there was no way he could change the past, no way he could *not* have grown up in a dysfunctional family, Andrew felt sorry for himself. He conned himself into believing that he was doomed to misery for the rest of his life. The truth was that he had found a convenient excuse to avoid the hard work of finishing the changes he had begun.

Confronting the truth about our own history is necessary for us to heal. Feelings of anger are very normal when we take an honest look at our childhoods and the dysfunctional families in which we were raised. So are feelings of sadness. Letting ourselves get caught in a cycle of blaming our families or self-pity, however, stops our growth.

When we accuse others of ruining our lives because of choices they made long ago, we remain stuck in the past, in our codependency. Like Andrew, we become convinced that we are unable to change. We give up our power to be happy and emotionally healthy human beings to events that happened years ago and to people who may have changed. We know that we learned to be codependent from our childhood experiences, but we're too busy with self-pity and making people pay for what they have done to us to have time or energy left over for learning *not* to be codependent.

LETTING GO TO GROW

Dealing with the past spent in a family that could not or would not meet our needs pushes us to go through a grieving process. The people who are important to us probably have not died, but our childhood has. If we are seriously working through our codependency, the false hope of being able to go back and have a happy childhood must die as well.

We can never go back and live it again to get it right. Our thoughts and emotions can turn back in time, and we can relive memories in our minds, but with every passing minute our lives are physically moving forward. When we do not allow ourselves to grieve, blame, bitterness, and self-pity set in.

To grow, we need to let go. Counselors who work with people who have suffered a loss, whether of a mate or a pet, a marriage or a job, identify several stages grieving people go through before they can fully accept their loss. Those stages seem to be the same for recovering codependents who are saying good-bye to the delusion that they can magically turn back the clock to the past. Recovering codependents go through five stages of grief:

Denial.   Codependents who are in denial may still want to see their dysfunctional families as perfectly healthy. Instead, they blame themselves for not getting what they needed when they were growing up. When we begin to understand how we were hurt by our childhood experiences, we often feel shocked or numb.

Anger.   When the shock wears off, most codependents feel a great deal of anger. They may be outraged at having been victims of neglect or of verbal, emotional, sexual, or physical abuse. During the first stages of their anger, recovering codependents more often than not are furious with their parents. In time, many are able to separate who their parents are from what they did or did not do in the past. It is possible to hate what happened to you in childhood without hating the people who did it.

Sadness.   As the anger starts to fade, codependents in recovery next feel sad because we never got to experience the happy childhood of kids raised in functional families. (Often our notion of a functional family is a fantasy picture. Healthy families have problems, too!) During this stage codependents may replay the past in their minds, thinking, "If only my parents had been different, if only Mom hadn't used drugs, if only my brother hadn't been born with a handicap—my life would be completely different today." Many times we feel a longing to return to being little kids.

Apathy.   When our sadness starts to leave us, we codependents often feel empty and drained of energy for a time. After all, sadness, anger, and resentment, whether suppressed or expressed, served as the center for our lives. New feelings begin to surface, and they can be confusing. We need to spend some quiet time with ourselves to sort things out. The past is gone and the future has not yet arrived. Even though it may not seem that much is happening on the outside, this stage enables us to better know and accept ourselves.

Acceptance. Eventually we codependents come to accept that we can do nothing to change our imperfect childhoods. Those experiences are part of us; they helped shape who we are today. When we stop hiding from our past or fighting it, those unhappy times lose their power to control us today. We are able to live in the present and to accept life moment by moment without needing to put on an act or to control people. We are able to make the choice to take charge of our lives.

Accepting our problem-filled childhoods is not the same as believing we deserved them or even pretending with our family members that they didn't happen. It is not the same as forgiveness either, although it may be a first step. Some codependents come to a place in their emotional growth at which they are ready to forgive their parents for failing to meet their needs. Others are not ready, and that's okay; they are doing what is best for them.

The grieving process needs to be lived through before we are able to forgive wholeheartedly. If we try to skip the anger stage by focusing too soon on understanding why our parents didn't meet our needs, we run the risk of remaining codependent—focusing on other people while ignoring ourselves. If we feel uncomfortable with sadness and decide not to experience our loss, we never make it to acceptance.

Progressing through the grief stages can at times be frustrating, and we may need to talk with a counselor or other professional if our progress seems to stop. But by allowing ourselves to work our way through saying good-bye to lost childhood rather than trying to force ourselves to change overnight, we ensure our recovery. Our healing may be slow, but it will be steady as we learn to live one day at a time firmly rooted in the present.

If the present becomes stressful, as it does sometimes for everyone, we can learn to cope by trying some of the following:

- Being gentle with ourselves and not pushing too hard.
- Forgiving ourselves when we make mistakes.
- Taking quiet time for ourselves.
- Getting enough sleep.
- Eating nutritionally balanced meals.
- Including some kind of physical activity in our lives.
- Making time for fun.
- Allowing time-outs from our problems by going to a movie, taking a nap, listening to music, or reading a book.
- Learning relaxation techniques such as deep breathing, meditation, and creative visualization.

SOLVING PROBLEMS/SETTING GOALS

When we live in the present and can manage our stress, we are able to begin to focus on how we want our lives to be. Waking up from codependency is a lot like waking up from a deep sleep. At first we may be confused and unsure of ourselves. It takes us longer than others to figure out what we're feeling and to think of appropriate ways to express those feelings. We have lived most of our lives reacting to the needs and wants of others. Now suddenly we realize that we are in control of how we handle our feelings and whether or not our needs are met. We are not used to that freedom. Taking charge means that we have a major responsibility for solving our problems and a major say in what we want to do and to become. This new way of living can bring us great joy; problem-solving can also be a challenge because we are not used to it.

Now that we are taking charge, we can no longer sit around waiting for others to rescue us and blaming them when they don't. It is up to us to figure out what has gone wrong and how to correct it. For instance, if your tennis racket is broken and you don't have money to buy a new one, you need to decide what to do about it rather than pout and hope someone will notice what's wrong and do something for you.

One of the first steps in problem-solving is to come up with as many solutions as you can, no matter how silly they may seem. Practicality doesn't count when you're brain-storming. Numbers do. You might come up with a list of ideas about how to get money that range from selling pencils on the street corner to calling up all of your relatives and offering to wash their cars. Getting an after-school job could be on the list as well as asking your parents for money. The more options you can come up with when you problem-solve, the greater are your chances of finding a solution that will work.

When you have finished your list, let it sit for a while. Some of our best ideas come when we sleep on our problems. If we release our frantic focus on coming up with an answer now, we free our subconscious to take over. When you have let the challenge cook in the back of your mind for a while, pull out your list and begin narrowing it down by crossing off the solutions you are fairly sure won't work and circling the best ones.

Check to see if there are any changes you can make so that an idea will work better. If your relatives don't need their cars washed but do have lots of kids, perhaps baby-sitting would be a better way to get the money. If you can't work weekdays because you're on a committee at school, you might see if you could get a job on weekends only. Maybe you could borrow part of the money.

Once you come up with a solution, it becomes a goal to be reached. For instance, if your problem was not having enough money for the racket and your solution was baby-sitting your cousins, your goal would be earning $100 by watching your aunts' and uncles' kids.

Sometimes during recovery we codependents sabotage ourselves by setting unreasonable goals, especially if we were perfectionistic to begin with. We might decide we have to earn the entire amount for the tennis racket by next week. Or we carry things many steps further and believe that since we are now emotionally healthy we ought to be able to get into Harvard Law School or be voted class president. Since we are in charge of our lives, we need to get a 4.0 grade point average or become head cheerleader.

Julie, who had been working through an unhappy childhood as the daughter of a father who sexually abused her before he abandoned the family, was making headway in her weekly therapy. The horrible nightmares she had had since childhood had stopped, and she was actually starting to feel good about herself. She had begun adding a little fun to her life instead of studying six hours a night. Some days she felt like a butterfly emerging from a cocoon.

Even though her mother and her teachers saw her transformation as a near miracle, Julie was frustrated. The big changes were not enough, she told herself; she *ought* to be losing weight and she *should* have a boyfriend. So she made up a list of goals: She would lose twenty pounds in a month, work out two hours a night, and be going steady by the end of the school year. Only when all that had been accomplished would she consider her recovery a success. Needless to say, her goals were impossibly high, and she made herself miserable.

If we spent our codependent years being underachievers, we may not even know how to set goals. We never had to make plans in the past because Mom was only going to get drunk and ruin them anyway, or Dad wanted to keep control and he set all our goals for us. In that case we say, "Oh, well, I'll never get a new tennis racket anyway, so why should I bother trying?"

Like any other challenge in codependency recovery, setting goals gets easier with practice. At the start we need to learn to set priorities. If we don't take time to decide which of our aims is most important to us, we bite off more than we can chew and then find we can accomplish little if anything.

We also need to keep in mind that the process of working toward the goal is a valuable learning experience for us. Actually the process can be far more important than the result. If we don't take joy in the journey toward our goals, we are tempted to give up before we give our growth a chance. Sometimes even after struggling for a long time, we are prevented by things beyond our control from doing what we want to do. Or maybe we do get where we thought we wanted to go only to find that it's not where we want to be at all. If the trip itself wasn't any fun, we wind up feeling bitter and disappointed.

Whether your goal is earning money for a racket, getting into college, finding a job, buying a car, or making friends, there are ways you can make the challenge easier.

GOAL-SETTING STRATEGIES

1. Write your goals down. When you have them in front of you, it's easier to decide whether or not you are trying to do too many things at once.
2. Decide which goals are most important to you. Those are the ones that should receive most of your time, energy, and attention.
3. Be sure your goals are realistic. Can you really expect to be a professional dancer by next year if you start lessons this week? Is it a healthy choice to try to lose ten pounds a week?
4. Divide your goals into short-term and long-term projects. You may be able to accomplish cleaning up your room in a few hours. Earning five hundred dollars for a class trip will take much longer. To reach your goals, you need to plan accordingly.
5. Separate your big goals into little steps and number them in the order you need to do them. A major project like going to college or trade school can be so overwhelming that you can't get to work on it. Sending away for catalogs today, setting up an appointment with your high school counselor tomorrow, and visiting one school next week are much easier to handle.
6. Be flexible about your goals. Maybe after you have taken a few small steps you decide that going to

beauty school is not your thing at all. In that case be willing to change direction.

COPING WITH COMPULSIONS AND ADDICTIONS

If we have relied on drugs, alcohol, or compulsive activities to fill the empty space inside, now as we try to cure our codependency we may find our recovery moving at a snail's pace. Counselors believe that codependency is at the bottom of many, if not most, addictive behaviors. Until we admit and do something about our addictions, any real growth is doomed to fail. Faithfully reading books, doing exercises, and even attending meetings will not work unless we first face up to our addictions and compulsions.

Among the ways teenagers try to escape the reality of their feelings and their dysfunctional families are the following:

Alcohol. Many teens experiment with drinking. They may have a couple of beers at a party or even get drunk once or twice to see how it feels. Problems arise when drinking becomes more than occasional and getting drunk becomes a habit. Even though heavy-drinking teenagers may not be alcoholics with a physical addiction, their irresponsible drinking can be a psychological dependency: Unless they are high, they don't feel good about themselves.

Drugs. From marijuana to crack and heroin, drugs alter the user's mood. Even a drug that is not physically addictive can cause big problems. When teenagers use drugs, they cover up deeper problems such as feeling unworthy, unloved, and ashamed. Most drugs cause us to withdraw into ourselves and live in a private fantasy world.

Before we can heal from our codependency, we need to reconnect with the real world.

Love and/or sex. The teenage years are a time for learning to form romantic relationships. Sometimes, though, we may escape into love or sex almost as if it were a drug. We must have a boyfriend or girlfriend because we are terrified of being alone, and we need a partner so that we can feel good about who we are. We may substitute sex for affection or emotional intimacy. In that instance, since it does not provide us with what we really need, we can get hooked on having one partner after another.

Food. Some people with eating disorders gorge on food to fill the empty space inside, their *emotional* hunger. Others stop eating in an effort to gain control over at least one area of their lives. In both cases food becomes the central focus of nearly every waking moment. Anorexia, bulimia, and overeating are not only female problems. Teenage boys can have them, too. In fact in sports like wrestling, eating disorders may be encouraged.

Shopping. "If only I had one more sweater or comic book or pair of shoes, *then* I'd be happy," is the lament of the compulsive shopper. People who try to make themselves feel good by obtaining things often find the strategy does not work. Then they need to buy more and more things. In time they may spend all their money and start borrowing to keep up their habit.

Thrill-seeking. Driving too fast, shoplifting, cheating on tests—thrill-seekers use such tactics to stay on the edge and feel the heady adrenaline rush that comes with getting away with something. They flirt with trouble and sometimes put their very lives in danger. In moments other people would call calm, thrill-seekers are bored. They seek out the stimulation of taking foolish risks much the way drug addicts take temporary pleasure in the substances they abuse.

In the beginning we may have used these methods occasionally to cope or to feel better, but for some of us they become ingrained habits that take on an existence of their own. Eventually they may take over our lives because we have lost the power to control them.

A substance or activity has stopped being something we like and enjoy quite often and has turned into an addiction or compulsion when:

- We need more and more of the substance or activity to be satisfied.
- Our lives are organized around it to the extent that our relationships, our schoolwork, and our other interests suffer.
- Instead of using the substance or activity to feel "high," we use it to feel normal.
- We can't imagine living without it.
- We tell ourselves we can stop at any time, but we don't.

Dealing with a compulsion or addiction is not something we can do very easily on our own, especially if it has been part of us for more than a short time. The wisest way to regain control is to seek professional help in the form of counseling. Support groups such as Alcoholics Anonymous can also ease our change to compulsion-free living. Suggestions for finding help and addresses of some support groups are given at the end of this book.

HELP, I'M HAVING AN IDENTITY CRISIS

When we recover from codependency, we don't do it in a vacuum. Most of the time teenagers who are healing are still living with their families. They attend the same school they did when they were codependents; they see the same people and have the same friends. Most of us feel very excited about the positive changes we are making. We feel shocked and betrayed that our families and friends may not view this transition to an independent life-style with the same enthusiasm we do. Even though they care about us, at times they seem to do everything they can to make us go back to the way we were.

> When Holly started feeling more self-confident, her friends called her stuck-up. Who did she think she was, joining clubs and wearing makeup? Did she think she was better than they were. When she stopped smoking marijuana, they threatened to drop her. Even her mother seemed uncomfortable around her since she stopped feeling angry all the time. Holly had thought that once she really communicated with her mother, their arguments would stop. But now, even though Holly didn't pick fights, her mother did. It seemed as if everyone in her life wanted her to be codependent again.

Often the people with whom we are closest do not welcome our recovery with open arms, and we end up feeling hurt and wanting to give up. The changes we are making may upset them for a variety of reasons. They are used to relating to us in old ways. When we change from the inside out, we force them to change the way they see us and act toward us. Any change, even a change for the better, is stressful. Some people simply don't know how to treat us now. Others get upset because seeing our transformations forces them to look at their own codependent behavior.

Healing from codependency can be especially tough for teenagers who still live at home and whose parents have authority over them. We can make new friends, but making a new family is not that easy. Family systems are often difficult to change without professional counseling. Sometimes the best recovering teens can do is to practice this new way of living with others *outside* of their families. That's good enough for now.

No matter how reluctant the people you know are to accept the new improved you, there are ways to keep yourself on the road to recovery:

- Don't push your recovery down others' throats or try to force them to change with you. They may not be ready. Besides, trying to reform others is controlling, codependent behavior!
- Try to spend time with others who are supportive of your recovery. They could be friends, a teacher, a counselor, or an organized support group. The buddy system works.
- Focus on your successes, even the small ones, and reward yourself for them. When we wait for other people to pat us on the back, we set ourselves up for disappointment.
- Be patient with yourself and with the other people in your life. Sometimes you *will* take a step back for every two steps forward on your recovery journey. Sometimes others *need* more time to adjust to the changes we're making. *Easy does it.*

HAPPILY EVER AFTER?

You have almost finished this book. If you have been thinking about what you read and working through the exercises, chances are you are starting to see some improvements in your life. You are beginning to like, respect, and trust yourself. You are able to open up and share with others. You can set boundaries. For the first time in ages you are starting to feel good about yourself, happy, high on life. If you are a typical recovering codependent, those joyful feelings may be a little strange.

Maybe you need to do one last exercise. Get a big piece of bright paper and make a sign for your room to remind yourself: "IT'S OKAY TO BE HAPPY!"

In fact, it is more than okay; it is essential to continued growth. Back in the dark ages of our codependency many of us were so used to feeling miserable that today we are uncomfortable when we feel too good. When we begin to fall into self-doubt and guilt because things are going too well, we have to remind ourselves that there is no such thing as being *too* happy or feeling *too* good. We deserve to make our lives the best they can be and to enjoy each day to the fullest.

A RECOVERING CODEPENDENT'S BILL OF RIGHTS

1. You have the right to be who you are and to feel good about yourself.
2. You have a right to think your own thoughts and to form your own values.
3. You have a right to make choices based on those values so long as you don't deliberately hurt others or yourself.

4. You have a right to feel your own feelings and to express them.
5. You have a right to recognize your own needs and to ask others to help you meet them, knowing that they have the right to refuse.
6. You have a right to respect as a human being, the right to be listened to, and the right to be loved.
7. You have a right to set mental, emotional, physical, and spiritual boundaries.
8. You have a right to make mistakes.
9. You have a right to ask questions and to learn.
10. You have a right to change and to grow.

Resources

Many self-help support groups exist to help codependents cope with the problems they face. You can find chapters that meet in your area by talking with a high school counselor or calling a mental health center. If your research does not turn up what you need, contact the national organizations listed below. Enclose a self-addressed, stamped envelope with your request, and they will send you information about meetings near where you live. Many of these groups publish informational pamphlets, so ask for a list of publications when you write.

CODEPENDENCY

Codependents Anonymous (CODA)
P.O. Box 33577
Phoenix, AZ 85067-3577

FOR TEENS WITH PROBLEM PARENTS

Alateen
Al-Anon Family Group Headquarters
P.O. Box 862, Midtown Station
New York, NY 10018-6106

National Association for Children of Alcoholics
31706 Coast Highway, Suite 201
South Laguna, CA 92677

Adult Children of Alcoholics
P.O. Box 35623
Los Angeles, CA 90035

Families Anonymous (Families of Substance Abusers)
P.O. Box 528
Van Nuys, CA 91408

COPING WITH OUR OWN ADDICTIONS AND COMPULSIONS

Anorexia Nervosa and Associated Disorders
P.O. Box 7
Highland Park, IL 60035

Overeaters Anonymous
P.O. Box 92870
Los Angeles, CA 90009

Narcotics Anonymous
P.O. Box 9999
Van Nuys, CA 91409

Alcoholics Anonymous
Box 459, Grand Central Station
New York, NY 10163

Further Reading

Beattie, Melody. *Beyond Codependency—And Getting Better All the Time.* San Francisco: Harper/Hazelden, 1989.

————. *Codependent No More.* San Francisco: Harper/Hazelden, 1987.

Berry, Carmen Renee. *When Helping Me Is Hurting You.* San Francisco: Harper & Row, 1988.

Bradshaw, John. *Bradshaw on the Family.* Deerfield Beach, FL: Health Communications, Inc., 1988.

————. *Healing the Shame That Binds You.* Deerfield Beach, FL: Health Communications, Inc., 1988.

Mellody, Pia. *Facing Codependence.* San Francisco: Harper & Row, 1989.

Namka, Lynne. *The Doormat Syndrome.* Deerfield Beach, FL: Health Communications, Inc., 1989.

Weinhold, Barry and Janae. *Breaking Free of the Codependency Trap.* Walpole, NH: Stillpoint Books, 1989.

Whitfield, Charles. *Healing the Child Within.* Deerfield Beach, FL: Health Communications, Inc., 1987.

Index